Twayne's English Authors Series

Sylvia E. Bowman, *Editor*

INDIANA UNIVERSITY

Douglas Jerrold

 146

Douglas Jerrold

By RICHARD M. KELLY
University of Tennessee

Twayne Publishers, Inc. :: New York

For Barbara

Preface

When one refers to the Great Exhibition of 1851 as the "Crystal Palace," he is indebted to the satirical imagination of Douglas Jerrold, who first created the name to poke fun at the Victorians' self-importance. Remembered today as the author of the play *Black-Eyed Susan* and of a serial, *Mrs. Caudle's Curtain Lectures,* Jerrold was nevertheless an outstanding wit, one of the most popular and prolific playwrights of his day, the man most responsible for the early success of *Punch,* the author of numerous short stories, sketches, essays, and novels, and a friend of Charles Dickens, William Makepeace Thackeray, and other prominent authors.

He has remained too long in the background of Victorian studies, and consequently his influence upon the development of the drama, upon the rise of comic journalism, and upon his famous contemporaries has gone unnoticed. Even more regrettable is the absence of his works from library shelves and from anthologies of Victorian literature, for he has written a number of comic masterpieces that deserve reading today.

Most of the work written about Jerrold has come from his family, friends, and admirers and is, therefore, marred by disproportionate praise. The time now seems ripe to take a close, hard look at him, to view him objectively and in perspective, and to study him thoroughly and critically as he deserves. After an introduction to his life and times, the focus of this critical-analytical study is upon his plays, his writings in *Punch,* and his miscellaneous essays, short fiction, and novels. Since many of Jerrold's works have not been collected and even his collected works are becoming prizes for rare book hunters, it is necessary to provide brief summaries of the works under consideration. In the absence of a modern biography of Jerrold, relatively little attention is given to details of his life. Fortunately, however, Michael Slater is planning a full-scale biography of Jerrold, a work which should fill a serious gap in the history of Victorian literature.

I am indebted to the following people for the generous assistance they have afforded me in my study: Arthur Adrian, John Bradley, Leslie Marchand, Oscar Maurer, Charles Richard Sanders, O. G. W. Stallybrass, and the librarian of *Punch*. I also extend my appreciation to the University of Tennessee Graduate School for a summer grant that expedited the completion of the manuscript. I especially want to thank Professor Lionel Stevenson, who directed my dissertation on Douglas Jerrold, and my wife, who suggested many helpful changes in the manuscript.

Finally, I gratefully acknowledge permission to use, in different form, my previously published essays: "Mrs. Caudle, a Victorian Curtain Lecturer," *University of Toronto Quarterly* (1969); "The American in England: an Examination of a Hitherto Neglected Satire by Douglas Jerrold," *Victorian Newsletter* (1967); and "Punch's Letters to His Son" (1967) and "Douglas Jerrold and William Makepeace Thackeray: the Jenkins Papers" (1970), *The Satire Newsletter*.

RICHARD M. KELLY

University of Tennessee

Contents

Contents

Chronology

1803   Douglas William Jerrold born in London, January 3; reared at Willsley, near Cranbrook, in Kent.

1807   Moves with his family to Blue Town, Sheerness.

1813   Through the influence of Captain Charles J. Austen, a brother of the novelist Jane Austen, Douglas is made a midshipman on the guardship *Namur*.

1815   Transferred in April to the brig *Earnest*, which conveyed transports to Ostend on the eve of Waterloo. Leaves service in October.

1816   Moves with his family to London; he works as a printer's apprentice.

1818   Writes his first play, *The Duellists*, which is rejected by English Opera House; finally produced in 1821 at Sadler's Wells under the new title, *More Frightened Than Hurt*.

1823   First contribution to a newspaper published in *Sunday Monitor*: a letter protesting the hawking of "dying speeches" of condemned criminals.

1824   Marries Mary Ann Swann, the daughter of a postal worker.

1825   Hired as salaried playwright for the Coburg Theatre by manager George Bowell Davidge. Contributes to the *Monthly Magazine*.

1829   First great theatrical success, *Black-Eyed Susan*, performed at the Surrey Theatre on June 8; it has record run of four hundred nights at six theaters the first year.

1831   Begins contributing to the *Athenaeum*.

1832   Publishes satiric papers in *Punch in London*, a short-lived early prototype of *Punch*. Wins first success at a licensed theater with *The Rent Day*, a domestic drama produced at Drury Lane on January 25.

1835   Goes to Paris where he first meets Thackeray and Henry Mayhew. Contributes to *Blackwood's Magazine* and the

Freemason's Quarterly. Meets Charles Dickens in Thistle Grove, Brompton.

1836 *The Painter of Ghent,* a tragedy, produced at the Strand Theatre, jointly managed by Jerrold and his brother-in-law, William Hammond.

1837 Begins writing for the *New Monthly Magazine.*

1838 Publishes *Men of Character,* his first work in volume form, composed of fictional sketches previously printed in *Blackwood's Magazine* and other periodicals.

1839 Publishes *The Handbook of Swindling;* edits *Heads of the People.*

1841 First contribution to *Punch,* "Punch and Peel," a satiric account of the Bedchamber Plot, appears in the magazine's second number above the signature "Q."

1842 *The Prisoner of War* produced at Drury Lane; *Bubbles of the Day* at Covent Garden. Publishes *Cakes and Ale,* a collection of previously published short stories and essays. Contributes *Punch's Letters to His Son* to *Punch.*

1843 *Punch's Letters to His Son* published in volume form. Contributes *The Story of a Feather* to *Punch.* Begins editing *The Illuminated Magazine,* in which he publishes *The Chronicles of Clovernook.*

1844 *The Story of a Feather* published in volume form. Contributes *Punch's Complete Letter Writer* to *Punch.*

1845 His most productive year. *Punch's Complete Letter Writer* appears in volume form. Contributes *Mrs. Caudle's Curtain Lectures* to *Punch.* Begins editing *Douglas Jerrold's Shilling Magazine,* in which he publishes his novel, *St. Giles and St. James. Time Works Wonders,* a comedy, produced at the Haymarket Theatre. Performs with Dickens in *Every Man in His Humour.*

1846 Contributes *Miss Robinson Crusoe* and *The English in Little* to *Punch. Mrs. Caudle's Curtain Lectures* and *The Chronicles of Clovernook* published in volume form. Begins editing *Douglas Jerrold's Weekly Newspaper.*

1847 Contributes *Capsicum House for Young Ladies* to *Punch.*

1848 Begins publication of his novel, *A Man Made of Money,* in monthly parts.

1849 Feuds with Dickens on the subject of capital punishment. The *Catspaw* produced at the Haymarket Theatre.

Chronology

1850   *The Sick Giant and the Doctor Dwarf* published in the *Illustrated London News.*

1851   His collected works begin to be published in weekly numbers from January, 1851, to June, 1854. *Retired From Business* produced at the Haymarket Theatre.

1852   Begins editing *Lloyd's Weekly Newspaper,* a job he retains until his death.

1853   Command performance of *St. Cupid* given at Windsor Castle on January 21. Contributes the serial *Our Honeymoon* to *Punch.*

1854   *A Heart of Gold* produced at the Princess's Theatre.

1856   Meets Nathaniel Hawthorne.

1857   Dies on June 8. Dickens and Thackeray give public readings of their works to help raise funds for Mrs. Jerrold and her unmarried daughter.

CHAPTER 1

Through Grub Street

IF Douglas William Jerrold were ever subjected to a curtain lecture by his wife or if he ever dreamed of becoming a great novelist or grieved for his sins, it will never be known. Like Robert Browning, Jerrold took great precaution not to reveal his personal life in his writings. Although both his son and grandson have written his biography, they concern themselves chiefly with external events; outwardly, Jerrold's life is an ordinary one. Therefore, the emphasis in this chapter is on the development of the man's career as a dramatist, an author, and a journalist.

Contained in one of Jerrold's stories is a romanticized character sketch of the strolling player as "the merry preacher of the noblest, grandest lessons of human thought," who "informs human clay with thoughts and throbbings that refine it." [1] This delineation fittingly describes his own father, Samuel Jerrold, who was once a member of the Dover Company of strolling players. If this group, which toured the area around Eastbourne, sometimes failed to elicit the adulation of the country audience, it was guaranteed applause whenever Samuel Jerrold donned his famous shoes before a performance, for they were none other than those of the renowned David Garrick.

Samuel eventually settled down to manage a small theater, which he converted from a barn, in Cranbrook. He and his wife, the former Miss Simpson, who had been an actress in the strolling company, lived nearby the theater in the small Kentish village of Willsley; and their first two children, Robert and Charles, were reared there. Robert later became an actor-manager like his father, and Charles chose a career in the Royal Navy. In 1794, several years after his wife's death, Samuel married a Miss Reid, a young actress about half his age. On January 3, 1803, during a brief visit to London, Mrs. Jerrold gave birth to a son, Douglas William. The family soon returned to the pastoral quiet of Cranbrook where young Douglas, because both his parents were frequently upon the stage, was reared by his maternal grandmother. In 1807, Mr. Jerrold acquired the lease for a theater in Blue Town, Sheerness; and his family had to exchange the peaceful countryside of Kent for the turmoil of a thriving seaport during a period of great naval activity. Two years earlier Viscount Horatio Nelson had won his great victory at Trafalgar and Thomas Dibdin's naval airs were adding to the general enthusiasm for the British Navy. The harbor of Blue Town was crowded with warships and transports, and sailors with their stories and ready money entertained and enriched its citizenry. It is little wonder, then, that young Douglas was soon to enlist in the navy and later wrote his popular nautical melodramas, which were filled with romanticized jolly jack tars and with patriotic naval songs.

Although Douglas attended a small school in Sheerness for a few years, he acquired most of his early learning from his solicitous grandmother and from an actor in his father's company. More interested in adventure stories and in natural history than in childhood games, he spent most of his time alone in the family library. In later life, reflecting upon these early days in Sheerness, he jokingly remarked that his only companion had been "the little buoy at the Nore." [2] He was introduced to the stage as a mere infant when the great actor of the day, Edmund Kean, carried him on stage in *Rolla*. Nevertheless, the splendor of the navy and not of the theater fired the imagination of the young boy. Four days before Christmas of 1813, at the tender age of ten, Douglas volunteered for service on the guardship *Namur*, anchored at the Nore. The ship's captain, Charles Austen, a brother of the novelist Jane Austen, was permissive enough to allow the boy to keep pet pigeons on board, as well as a small library which served to further the youth's education. Douglas quickly befriended foremastman Clarkson Stanfield, and they produced small theatricals to offset the monotonous routine aboard ship. The tedium soon passed when in 1815 the war with France was reaching a climax; Douglas was then transferred to the gunbrig *Earnest,* which transported wounded soldiers from the battlefield at Waterloo to Ostend. Although he never engaged in actual combat, the ghastly sights of bleeding and dying Englishmen instilled in the midshipman a hatred for war and for the Frenchmen that later found expression in his essays for *Punch.* He also saw his own shipmates flogged until unconscious for acts of disobedience, the memories of which served him later in his ceaseless campaigns against man's inhumanity to man.

When Douglas left the service and returned to his parents' home, he discovered, now that the peace had come and had depopulated the small seaport town, that his father's theatricals were failing. At the close of the year, the family moved to London, where Mrs. Jerrold and her two daughters obtained employment as actresses, while Mr. Jerrold, a much disappointed and tired old man, stayed at home reading to his son. In an effort to contribute his share in helping to pay the family's expenses, Douglas became a printer's apprentice and quickly learned the mechanics of book publishing, a first step toward his career in journalism and editorship. He rose early in the mornings to study his Latin grammar or to read Shakespeare, and he devoured the novels of Sir Walter Scott in snatches during his twelve-hour workday and in the evenings. He also took advantage of his spare hours to attend the famous London playhouses where he saw the great actors of the day—Edmund Kean, John Kemble, and Charles Matthews.

In 1818, Douglas wrote his first play, a farce entitled *The Duellists,* and sent it to the English Opera House where it remained unread for two years. The piece was finally accepted after three years by Sadler's Wells. Rechristened *More Frightened Than Hurt,* it enjoyed a popular success that led to subsequent productions in Paris and at Madame Vestris' Olympic Theatre. The nineteen-year-old author must have been greatly pleased with his initial success, for he followed it quickly with two spectacular melodramas, *The Chieftain's Oath* and *The Gipsy of Derncleugh.*

After the printing shop at which he was working failed, Jerrold became a compositor for the *Sunday Monitor.* His future reputation as a social reformer was forecast by a letter he had published in the *Monitor* protesting the custom of hawking the "dying speeches" of condemned criminals: "Amongst the many prevalent nuisances which call for a speedy redress, none, I think, are more conspicuous than the disgusting and I may say inhuman practice followed on every melancholy occasion when justice and the public welfare demand as an awful example the life of a fellow being —I advert to the custom of reading what are termed Dying Speeches." [3] In 1823, he began a series of critical descriptions of the popular actors of the day for John Duncombe's bimonthly *Mirror of the Stage.* That same year he wrote and had successfully produced at Sadler's Wells a new drama called *The Smoked Miser.*

Jerrold's future reputation as a radical liberal was anticipated in this year by a romantic scheme he devised with his friend Laman Blanchard. The two ardent young men planned to join Lord Byron in Greece to help the cause of liberty threatened by the Turkish tyrants. The idea was soon relinquished, however, in favor of practicality. On August 15, 1824, Jerrold married Mary Ann Swann, the daughter of a postal worker. Their marriage appears to have been happy and peaceful, although, outside of the fact that she bore him seven children, nothing is known about her.

In the autumn of 1826, Jerrold began publishing a number of colorful sketches of English characters and places in the *Monthly Magazine,* one of the leading monthlies of the day. That same year he was editing and writing for a Sunday journal called the *Weekly Times.* Meanwhile, he was also writing plays in rapid succession as salaried playwright for the Coburg Theatre. Still unable to get his plays produced at the patent houses, he had to content himself with outrageously small fees from the Coburg's ruthless taskmaster, George Bowell Davidge, for whom he wrote a total of seven plays, including *Fifteen Years of a Drunkard's Life, Ambrose Gwinett,* and *Martha Willis.*

Jerrold soon quarreled with Davidge, left the Coburg, and began writing for the Surrey Theatre, managed by Robert William Elliston, the actor-manager immortalized in Charles Lamb's famous essay. Here Jerrold achieved his first great theatrical success when on June 8, 1829, *Black-Eyed Susan; or, "All in the Downs"* made its debut. The play was enthusiastically received and enjoyed a near record run of four hundred nights at six theaters during its first year. Nevertheless, Jerrold's share in the profits amounted to a mere sixty pounds, ten of which were obtained by selling the copyright.

The success of the play, however, brought him a reputation as a brilliant young dramatist, and before the year was out, he was given the opportunity to write for the two patent houses, Drury Lane and Covent Garden. As a writer for the minor theaters, he had been, for most part, ignored by the critics: now he came under their scrutiny and was warmly praised. The audiences at these large theaters were accustomed to conventional melodramas adapted from the French, spectaculars, and roaring farces. When it was suggested to Jerrold that he should adapt a piece for Drury Lane, he replied emphatically, "I will come into this theatre as an original dramatist or not at all." [4] He insisted on writing an English play about an English theme, and he refused to adapt his play to the taste of the audience. Instead of spectacle and uproar, he dared to introduce silence upon the stage by writing most of the second act as a dumb show. Consequently, his debut at the patent theater with *The Witchfinder* was a miserable failure, and the play was removed from the boards after the first night. The failure made him apprehensive about producing his next play at Covent Garden, and he decided to give it instead to the Surrey, whose audience he knew well.

After a quarrel over finances with Elliston, Jerrold left the employ of the Surrey, had a successful performance of *The Devil's Ducat* at the Adelphi, and proceeded to establish himself in the licensed theaters with his comedy *The Bride of Ludgate* (1831) at Drury Lane. At this time, he again turned to journalism and published a series of attacks upon government and society in the *Athenaeum*. From 1831 to 1833, when Charles Lamb was contributing poems and essays, Jerrold used the pages of the magazine to assail the game laws, war, dishonest lawyers, and religious hypocrisy.

Independent comic journalism was somewhat of a novelty in 1831 when Gilbert à Becket and Henry Mayhew founded *Figaro in London*, a paper which poked fun at the passing events of popular interest. A number of imitative journals followed, including the penny-paper *Punch in London*, in which Jerrold ridiculed snobbery, toadyism, and humbug. Unlike *Figaro*, which continued for eight years, *Punch in London* expired after a few weeks. Nevertheless, these journals have historical importance, for out of them arose the new genre of comic journalism and *Punch*.

By the next year, Jerrold had written *The Rent Day*, which extended his fame among the critics and audiences of the licensed theaters. Despite the fact that the Examiner of Plays, George Colman, censored all of Jerrold's *damns*, *Gods*, and *heavens*, the play was very successful and brought a small fortune to the Drury Lane management.

Sometime during this year Jerrold, convalescing from a serious attack of rheumatism, first met Charles Dickens, then a reporter on the *Morning Chronicle.* Dickens recorded his impressions of the meeting: "I remember very well that when I first saw him in about the year 1835—when I went into his sick room in Thistle Grove, Brompton, and found him propped up in a great chair, bright-eyed and quick and eager in spirit, but very lame in body, he gave me the impression of tenderness. It never became dissociated from him." [5] The meeting proved to be eventful, for the young men were to become close, lifelong friends.

By the end of 1835, no less than thirteen new plays by Jerrold were produced at the best theaters in London. The warm reception accorded his romantic comedy *Doves in a Cage* (1835) reassured Jerrold that his goal to restore native drama to the English stage was being realized. The setting of the Fleet Prison and the allusions to West End, Newgate, Temple Gardens, and other well-known London landmarks testify to the indigenous nature of the play. More important than his creation of local atmosphere, however, is Jerrold's ability to wean audiences from mindless spectaculars to a verbal theater. Subsequent playwrights may owe him a debt of gratitude for helping to reverse the trend toward theatrical barbarism. A week after the play opened, Jerrold expressed his confidence in the theater public:

The cordiality with which this little play has been received by an audience (and an Adelphi Audience!) may afford a promise of better days to the despairing English dramatist, at present all but excluded from his native stage by foreign music and translated spectacle. It is manifest, that even an attempt, however feebly executed, to trust to the simplicity of comedy—depending neither upon the glories of the scene-painter, nor the cunning of the machinist—will be encouragingly accepted by the theatrical public, continually libelled as caring for nothing save processions and panoramas—steeds of neighing flesh and steeds of "bronze"; to be delighted only when the mask of comedy is exchanged for a masquerade, and the bowl of tragedy enlarged into a brazen cauldron. [6]

Between plays Jerrold began writing a number of amusing episodic stories for *Blackwood's Magazine* and whimsical tales and poems for the *Freemason's Quarterly Review.* Shortly thereafter, in 1836, he became theatrical critic for *The Constitutional and Public Ledger,* a liberal newspaper edited by his old friend Laman

Blanchard, and for which Thackeray was then writing news notes from Paris.

Jerrold ventured into the dual role of actor-manager when he and his brother-in-law, William John Hammond, jointly assumed the management of the Strand Theatre. Jerrold produced and acted in a few of his own plays, but he failed to distinguish himself in the new enterprise.

Early in 1838 he produced his first work in volume form. The fictional sketches he had written earlier for *Blackwood's Magazine* were issued in three volumes as *Men of Character,* with water color illustrations by Thackeray. This collection was followed by *The Handbook of Swindling* (1839), in which Jerrold attacks the hypocrisy of current morality by ironically describing how a swindler may best succeed in the world. Written under the pseudonym of Barabbas Whitefeather, the book's true authorship was never revealed during Jerrold's lifetime.

The year 1841 is notable in Jerrold's career, for it marks the beginning of his long and fruitful association with *Punch*. Since this topic is discussed in a later chapter, let it suffice to say that, despite his long commitment to *Punch,* Jerrold still managed to write many successful plays, to edit and write for a number of magazines and newspapers, and to enliven several important literary clubs with his wit.

The following year *The Prisoner of War* was produced at Drury Lane and achieved a distinct success. Three weeks later a second comedy, *Bubbles of the Day,* appeared at Covent Garden. At this time, two of Jerrold's best comedies were playing simultaneously at two of London's most distinguished theaters, when only a decade before both houses were closed to him.

A collection of essays entitled *Punch's Letters to His Son,* which Jerrold had been contributing to *Punch* during 1842, was published the following year in volume form. In an attempt to reach a still wider audience, he founded and edited the *Illuminated Magazine,* dedicated to the "masses of the people." The color implied in the title of the magazine was limited to the title page; and, although it was crudely reproduced, it was a notable experiment in the use of color illustrations. Jerrold was the first to recognize the talent of Wilkie Collins, who made his literary debut in the *Illuminated* with his story "The Last Stage Coachman." One issue brought Englishmen up-to-date on American history through a detailed pictorial and historical account of the bowie knife. As a contributor to the magazine, Jerrold's account of a utopian society entitled "The Chronicles of Clovernook" elicited praise from some discerning critics. Before setting out on his trip to Switzerland, Dickens informed Jerrold that the hermit-hero of Clovernook "took my fancy mightily . . . and I have stowed him away in the left-hand breast-pocket of my travelling-coat, that we may hold pleasant converse together on the Rhine." [7]

Jerrold left the *Illuminated Magazine* in 1844 for a more ambitious project. With the financial support of the publishers of *Punch*, he brought forth *Douglas Jerrold's Shilling Magazine*. The periodical was an innovation in publishing, for it broke away from the standard half crown then charged for such monthly miscellanies. The low price was in keeping with the stated purpose of the magazine, "that it shall appeal to the hearts of the Masses of England." As a contributor, Jerrold published in it his novel of social protest, *St. Giles and St. James,* in monthly installments. He also wrote about social and political events of the day in a series of satiric papers entitled "The Hedgehog Letters."

The year 1845 proved to be one of the most fruitful in Jerrold's career. Besides his work for the *Shilling Magazine,* he had published in volume form *Punch's Complete Letter Writer,* one of the most popular series in *Punch*. His comedy *Time Works Wonders* was successfully produced at the Haymarket. But his new serial for *Punch, Mrs. Caudle's Curtain Lectures,* was by far his most popular and significant work of the year, the one for which he is most often remembered today. Jerrold even found time during 1845 to act in a play containing a most unusual cast of amateurs. A group of literary men, including Dickens, John Forster, John Leech, and Mark Lemon, joined efforts in performing Ben Jonson's *Every Man in His Humour*. Although this company, known as the "Splendid Strollers," continued to give performances, Jerrold felt uncomfortable upon the stage and did not make many subsequent appearances with the group.

Jerrold performed best at conversation where his wit was given free play. Many of his contemporaries considered him to be the greatest wit of his age. Thackeray is reported to have claimed Jerrold to be the wittiest man he had ever known. Even in the present day, Gordon N. Ray has described Jerrold as "an authentic wit, after Sidney Smith, the most notable of his age. . . ." [8] He was praised for his repartee in his conversation more than in his writing, and it seems that everyone who ever knew him has contributed to the fund of remembered *bons mots* by Jerrold. For example, on one occasion, when there had been a heated discussion, a potential peace-maker broke in with, "Gentlemen, all I want is common sense—" "Exactly," interrupted Jerrold, "that is precisely what you *do* want." [9] And the argument ended in laughter. When a friend asked why the poet John Heraud always had dirty hands, Jerrold's explanation was "From his habit of constantly putting them up to his face." [10] When Jerrold was asked by Heraud, "Have you seen my *Descent into Hell?*," he replied, "No, but I should like to." [11] His sarcasm was so irrepressible that he was hardly less trenchant in speaking of his own wife. When she had reached middle age, he jokingly told her that he "wished wives were like bank notes, so that one of forty could be changed into two of twenty." Asked on another occasion who was dancing with her, he replied, "Some member of the Humane Society." [12] Jerrold exhibits the same kind of cleverness as Oscar Wilde, both men having uttered and written enough witticisms to call forth collections of their humorous dicta on topics ranging from marriage to literature.

For all his wit, Jerrold was intensely earnest in his radical journalism. In an attempt to secure more freedom in his political and social commentary, he established his own newspaper. The editor's opening article for *Douglas Jerrold's Weekly Newspaper* contained the welcome of a radical to Lord John Russell and the Whigs for the hope they offered to the poor and oppressed of England. Writing to Dickens shortly after the newspaper was started, Jerrold explained his need for independence:

This newspaper, with *other* allotments, is hard work; but it is *independence*. And it was the hope of it that stirred me to the doing. I have a feeling of dread—a something almost insane in its abhorrence of the condition of the old, worn-out literary man; the squeezed orange (*lemons* in my case, sing some sweet critics); the spent bullet; the useless lumber of the world, flung upon literary funds while alive, with the hat to be sent round for his coffin and his widow. And therefore I set up this newspaper, which—I am sure of it—you will be glad to learn, is a large success. [13]

A member of many clubs all his life, Jerrold established the Whittington Club in 1847 and began a small social revolution by allowing women to join the group on an equal basis with men. He attacked the double standard, calling the Englishman "a very good Christian sort of person at home, and at the same time little better than a Turk at his club." [14]

Early in 1849 Dickens gave a dinner to celebrate the beginning of the publication of *David Copperfield*. Although Jerrold was present among the illustrious company, which included Thomas Carlyle, Thackeray, and Mrs. Elizabeth Gaskell, only a few months later he and Dickens had a falling out. Radically opposed to capital punishment, Jerrold believed that Dickens had compromised his position when he favored private hanging over public execution. He wrote a heated note to Dickens: "In the meantime my Tom Thumb voice must be raised against any compromise that, in the sincerity of my opinion, shall tend to continue the hangman amongst us, whether in the Old Bailey street, or in the prison press-yard." A number of months later, when Jerrold happened to be eating dinner at a club Dickens walked in and took his seat without saying a word to his old friend. A few moments passed and Jerrold wheeled his chair around and exclaimed, "For God's sake let us be friends again! Life's not long enough for this!" [15]

After five years of absence from the stage, Jerrold produced his comedy *The Catspaw* at the Haymarket. If he was gratified by the success of his play, he was greatly annoyed by a passage in Leigh Hunt's *Autobiography* claiming that Jerrold's popularity in *Punch* was the chief reason the theaters welcomed his plays. Since he had over fifty plays to his credit before joining *Punch*, Jerrold's sense of injustice is easily understood. Set in 1850, the year of its representation, the play deals with a wealthy widow and her appealing legacy that involves her in a tedious Chancery suit. One wonders if Dickens saw the performance or read the text, for only two years later he chose a similar theme for his novel *Bleak House*.

From January, 1851, to June, 1854, a collected edition of Jerrold's writings was issued in weekly numbers of sixteen pages each, in monthly parts, and finally, in volumes. His novel, *A Man Made of Money*, and two new comic plays, *Retired From Busi-*

ness (1851), a keen satire on middle-class snobbery, and *St. Cupid* (1853), which was given a command performance at Windsor Castle, were included among his collected writings. In an attempt to revitalize his *Weekly Newspaper* by enlisting the services of a popular liberal, editor Edward Lloyd asked Jerrold to take over the editorship. Busily engaged in writing for *Punch,* Jerrold hesitated to accept the offer until Lloyd announced the annual salary to be one thousand pounds. From 1852 until his death five years later, Jerrold's radical political leaders and conscientious editing increased the circulation of *Lloyd's Weekly* to a record high.

Political unrest on the Continent, meantime, had long captured the imagination and sympathy of most English liberals; and, when the Hungarian patriot Louis Kossuth was in London, Jerrold proposed a penny subscription by which the works of Shakespeare could be purchased and presented to Kossuth as a token of England's esteem for this freedom fighter. The project was carried out successfully, and at the London Tavern Jerrold made a presentation speech in which he expressed the hope "that the day will come when you shall sit again at your own fireside in your own liberated Hungary . . . that sometimes turning the leaves of these word-wealthy volumes, you will think of Englishmen as a people who had for you and for your cause the warmest admiration and deepest sympathy. . . ." [16] His long, impassioned speech seemed a culmination of the thousands upon thousands of words he had written in defense of freedom during his long career as a journalist.

Perhaps the best portrait of Jerrold in his old age is that given by Nathaniel Hawthorne. When the noted American novelist visited London in 1856, he dined one evening with Charles Mackay and Jerrold at the illustrious Reform Club. Hawthorne recorded his experience in a diary, which reads in part as follows:

He was a very short man, but with breadth enough and a back excessively bent—bowed almost to deformity; very gray hair, and a face and expression of remarkable briskness and intelligence. His profile came out pretty boldly, and his eyes had the prominence that indicates, I believe, volubility in speech, nor did he fail to talk from the instant of his appearance, and in the tone of his voice, and in his glance, and in the whole man, there was something racy—a flavour of the humourist. His step was that of an aged man, and he put his stick down very decidedly at every footfall; though, as he afterwards told me, he was only fifty-two, he need not yet have been infirm.[17]

The distinct features which impressed Hawthorne had long provided the *Punch* artists with an easy subject for caricature. John Tenniel's sketches of Jerrold strike one as the prototype of the Mad Hatter, and unquestionably Jerrold inspired many of the drawings of Mr. Punch, the impish personification of the magazine.

Only a week before he died, on June 8, 1857, Jerrold was busily engaged in writing a nautical melodrama and in editing *Lloyd's*. Almost every literary and artistic celebrity in London was present among the two thousand mourners. His pallbearers included such distinguished men as Thackeray, Dickens, Richard Monckton Milnes, John Forster, Sir Joseph Paxton, Mark Lemon, and Horace Mayhew.

Jerrold died intestate, leaving his wife and daughter with what little money accrued from royalties on his plays and books. Consequently, a number of friends and admirers decided to raise money to help his family. Both Dickens and Thackeray gave readings of their works and donated the proceeds to the fund. Dickens read *A Christmas Carol* on June 30 at St. Martin's Hall; and three weeks later Thackeray read *Week-Day Preachers* at the same location. After all expenses were paid, a sum of two thousand pounds was left, which was invested by the trustees for the Jerrold family. The awful dread which Jerrold confided to Dickens ten years earlier had come to pass—"the hat to be sent around for his coffin and his widow."

CHAPTER 2

The Heyday of Melodrama

UNTIL 1843 there were only three legitimate, or royal, theaters in London: Drury Lane, Covent Garden, and the Haymarket. The Licensing Act of 1737, which allowed these theaters to monopolize conventional drama, permitted other establishments to present musicals, dances, and singing. Gradually there arose a species of drama called the "burletta," a play with enough song and dance interspersed to meet the requirements of the law. The royal theaters were soon abandoning the traditional drama in order to compete with the success of burlettas, spectacles, animal shows, and extravaganzas featured at the minor theaters.

With the gradual decline of the traditional verse drama in the early nineteenth century, the farce, burlesque, extravaganza, and melodrama enjoyed a period of great popularity. Although Jerrold attempted almost every type of play, from tragedy to dumb show, he excelled at farce and melodrama—two forms which the Victorian audience particularly craved. At a time when the lives of the middle class were being ruled by the merciless routine of the factory or shop, the melodrama offered them an escape into a world of thrilling excitement peopled by men and women often representing their own walks of life, a world that did not upset their expectations, and one which frequently preached the value of a virtuous life. The villain who is always punished and the heroine who always lives happily ever after were part of the formula for successful melodrama. The Victorians—a people who delighted in reading sermons and who understood and felt poverty and injustice—could easily appreciate the prescriptive morality and the poetic justice of the melodrama that eventually emerged after the thrills subsided.

Since there were no copyright laws to protect dramatists, a great many plays were translations or adaptations from the

French. As long as London theaters could be easily filled with warmed-over Paris successes that enriched managers and hack authors alike, there was little incentive for original English drama. The great size and poor lighting of the theaters helped to determine the style of acting during the first half of the nineteenth century. The Coburg Theatre, for example, seated four thousand people and required the actor to exaggerate all his gestures and to speak in stentorian tones if he were to be heard by all or even be seen in the candlelit auditorium. The declamatory and melodramatic styles of such famous actors as John Philip Kemble and Edmund Kean demanded scripts that allowed them to swell the house with passionate outbursts and to sweep across the stage in the grand manner. Moreover, the nature of a typical theater audience required plays with a bold, clear center of attention; for the star had to compete with prostitutes openly soliciting their patrons; with sandwich-eating, apple-munching workingmen; and with reeling, rowdy drunks. Samuel Jerrold's theater in Sheerness even entertained smugglers, who during one performance managed to hide eighty casks of gin under the floorboards. The pattern for melodrama was soon established, and every villain was destined to rant and scowl; and every heroine, to weep and faint.

The chief actor was frequently also the manager of the playhouse, a state of affairs that, for awhile, made the star system inevitable. Authors often wrote plays especially for men like Kean and Macready in which the rest of the cast merely acted as foils for their brilliance. Such an arrangement, while giving ample scope to the talents of the star, militated against the cooperation of the entire cast, which was not even needed for rehearsal.

I   Black-Eyed Susan

In spite of his prodigious output of journalism and fiction, Jerrold managed to write and have produced almost seventy plays. After Jerrold's mild initial success with *More Frightened Than Hurt* (1818) and others within the next few years, George Bowell Davidge, manager of the Coburg Theatre, hired the young dramatist as a full-time writer for his theater. While Jerrold received only a few pounds a week for his labors, the manager made a small fortune. Among the plays Jerrold supplied Davidge were

The Living Skeleton (1825), *London Characters* (1825), *Popular Felons* (1826), *Paul Pry* (1826), *Descart: the French Buccaneer* (1828), *The Tower of Lochlain, or the Idiot Son* (1828), *Wives by Advertisement* (1828), *Ambrose Gwinett* (1828), *Two Eyes Between Two* (1828), and *Fifteen Years of a Drunkard's Life* (1828). As the titles indicate, most of these pieces were either melodramas or farces, and they were all dashed off for a manager who was eager to please an audience whose enthusiasm was matched only by its lack of taste. Jerrold's last play for Davidge, *Fifteen Years of a Drunkard's Life*, is notable, however, for its attempt to convey a serious social and moral message. The drunkard Vernon is the real hero of this domestic melodrama, and the villain Glanville eloquently moralizes upon the evils of intoxication as the source of every crime.

After an argument with Davidge, Jerrold left the Coburg Theatre to work for Robert William Elliston, actor-manager for the Surrey Theatre. His third play for Elliston brought great fame to Jerrold and considerable wealth to his employer where on June 8, 1829, *Black-Eyed Susan; or, "All in the Downs"* made its debut. The nautical melodrama employs the plot of the villainous landlord threatening for his rent. William, the sailor-husband of Susan, comes home to find his wife about to be evicted from their cottage by Dograss, her uncle and landlord. Dograss, who has dealings with a group of smugglers, concocts the story of William's death in hopes of getting one of the smugglers to marry Susan, thereby assuring himself of a firm connection with the criminals. The fleet docks, and William arrives at his cottage just as his death is being announced to Susan. Meanwhile, William's captain comes on the scene in a state of drunkenness, assaults Susan, and is struck down by William.

At the court-martial, William is found guilty of striking a superior officer; and the noose is around his neck when the captain rushes on stage to announce that William is innocent of the crime. It happened that he had earlier applied for his discharge and the official document granting his request had been kept back by the villainy of Dograss, so that William was not in the king's service when he struck his officer. In the interval, the smugglers are captured by Lieutenant Pike and his troop of marines; and Dograss, who was in a small boat to attend the court-martial proceedings, grew so eager to hear William's death sentence that he slipped overboard and drowned.

The loose, episodic structure of the play was a characteristic of melodrama during the first half of the nineteenth century. Audiences enjoyed a stage bristling with activity, and playwrights crammed all the action they could into their plays. Jerrold, for example, added the episode with the smugglers to an early version of the play containing only three plots. Dograss' attempt to turn out Susan, Hatchet's plan to marry her, and William's court-martial present distinct story lines; and, since there is no rational connection between them, the addition of still another intrigue proved easy.

The play contains all the ingredients of the successful melodrama. The villain announces his villainy and acts only as a villain. The hero and heroine (an orphan ingenue) are hopelessly good, and they incorporate in their speech and behavior all the Sunday school and domestic virtues. The theme of sobriety as a prerequisite to morality is taken over from *Fifteen Years of a Drunkard's Life* and embodied in Captain Crosstree who, although he accosts Susan when he is drunk, is nevertheless a responsible officer of noble intentions when he is sober. The domestic scenes reflect the lower middle-class ideal of happiness represented by a comfortable cottage surrounded by green meadows and sheep. The sailor-husband's devotion to his wife is undaunted and Susan's long suffering and adamantine chastity overcome Hatchet's sinister designs. Jerrold's approach to lust is delicately handled in the scene where Captain Crosstree attempts to seduce Susan. Just as his passion is aroused beyond his control, William strikes him down. The threats to morality are balanced by the tearfully pathetic scene of the condemned William who, as a good sailor, stoically accepts his fate. He distributes some keepsakes to his shipmates and accompanies each souvenir with a sentimental account of its value. In his tearful farewell to Susan, he reflects upon their youthful love spent amidst a pastoral bower.

The popularity of robber bands and mysterious caverns, inspired by the German dramatist August von Kotzebue, contributed to the episode with the smugglers who dwell in dimly lit caves full of subterraneous passageways. Jerrold also capitalized upon the popularity of the British dancing and singing sailors, the "jolly tars." Following Britain's success in her naval wars, sailors came to be welcomed in taverns at the turn of the century. Actors then began to dress like sailors and to put on skits featuring idealized versions of the happy-go-lucky jack tar. The character was taken over by playwrights and conventional plots arose, the most common being that in which the sailor's wife is sexually threatened while he is away at sea.

Although Jerrold was not the first to present the jolly jack tar upon the stage, his characterization of William outshone any of his predecessors, established the character as a national trademark, and led the way for W. S. Gilbert's nautical operettas. Echoes of William's sailor talk are heard in comedies even today. For example, William's stylized diction is apparent in his lines after he discovers Hatchet and Raker telling Susan that he is dead: "Damn it, I'm running over at the scuppers, or you lubbers I'd been aboard of you before this. What! hang out false signals to the petticoat—may you both have the yellow flag over you, and go up in the smoke of the forecastle-chaser! Bring to a minute, and I'll be yard-arm and yard-arm with you, Susan, Susan! see, you swabs, how you've brought the white into her pretty figurehead (*puts* Susan *aside*—draws his cutlass.) Now, then, I'll make junk of one of you." [1]

II Thomas à Becket

Irritated at the large number of plays adopted from the French for the English stage, Jerrold determined to write an English play; and he produced *Thomas à Becket*, which, despite its failure at the Surrey, was his most successful attempt at historical drama. Written in an ambitious style, and freighted with pseudo-Elizabethan diction, the piece was brightened by the splendor of royal and ecclesiastical properties, by the powerful argument between Henry and Becket, and by Becket's spectacular martyrdom as the curtain falls.

Jerrold's theme is the danger to the state that results when the church usurps civil rights: the clergy become arrogant and corrupt and the lay people suffer the injustices of a clerical tyranny. Becket is portrayed as a great but misguided man whose death perpetuated for a while longer the church's encroachments on man's freedom. Jerrold makes his play a vehicle to deplore the rigidity of legalistic interpretation of doctrine to the detriment of human love, to expose a decadent and immoral clergy, and to present a specific instance of a wicked monk who, under the jurisdiction of the ecclesiastical courts, is given the benefit of powerful protection of the hierarchy and almost unchecked opportunity for rapaciousness.

Although the episodes dealing with Becket are, for the most part, historically accurate, in order to illustrate his theme Jerrold focuses much of the play upon a fictitious love story in which the monk is the villain. Lucia Vincent has fled from her household where she was unprotected from the advances of Philip de Brois, an evil monk who had been her tutor. Philip throws himself under the Archbishop's protection and convinces Thomas that Lucia had tempted him. Lucia immediately marries her lover, Walter Breakspear, and incurs the wrath of Thomas, who has been convinced by Philip that Lucia has broken vows of a nun in doing so. Becket threatens the pair with excommunication. Gradually, however, he becomes assured of Lucia's innocence and begins to experience painful doubt concerning Philip's honesty; but before he can resolve the problem he is murdered in the cathedral by the monks following King Henry's angry order.

Even though Jerrold was unsympathetic with Thomas' position and does not attempt to present him as a saint, he does give a sympathetic view of him as a man who has known failure after great success and who yet remains firm in his beliefs even after all personal satisfaction has gone out of his life. While the murder of Becket was an unfortunate event, the real tragedy, Jerrold implies, was that his claims for church precedence thereby received a few more years' grace in the reaction that followed.[2]

The serious theme and the unnatural diction of the characters in *Becket* did not strongly appeal to the audience of the illegitimate Surrey. Jerrold reverted, therefore, to farce and melodrama with *Sally in Our Alley* (1830), *Gervase Skinner* (1830), *The Mutiny at the Nore* (1830), and *The Press Gang* (1830), the last two plays revealing his lifelong interest in naval themes. He experimented with blank verse in *The Devil's Ducat; or the Gift of Mammon* (1830), but the real appeal of the play arises from the fascination about a diabolic coin which can never be spent no matter how frequently used for purchases. Social criticism, which begins to appear for the first time since *Fifteen Years of a Drunk-*

ard's Life, is aimed at corrupt lawyers and at hypocritical church-men.

George Colman, the Examiner of Plays, refused to license *The Bride of Ludgate* (1831) because it showed the merry King Charles in the disguise of a clergyman making advances to the pretty young wife of a merchant. When Jerrold simply changed the disguise to the habit of a lawyer, the play was allowed to be performed at Drury Lane. Welcomed now by the licensed theaters, Jerrold was becoming not only more successful but respectable. His next play for Drury Lane, *The Rent Day,* became his most popular drama after *Black-Eyed Susan* and established a record profit for that theater.

III The Rent Day

The domestic melodrama, a play dealing with the problems of the common man and his family, was in vogue during the middle of the century; and Jerrold's *The Rent Day* (1832) was one of the most popular plays of this type. He derived the idea for the piece from copies of the two celebrated paintings of Sir David Wilkie that hung on his study wall. The opening scene was presented as an exact reproduction of one of the paintings, and the artist, who was present at the opening night performance, was reduced to tears by the enthusiastic ovation given by the audience when the curtain was raised on his painting that had come to life.

The official harassment playwrights had to suffer is well exemplified by a memorandum sent to Jerrold by the Examiner of Plays only two days before the first performance of *The Rent Day*:

January 23, 1832. Please to omit the following underlined words in the representation of the drama called *The Rent Day*. Act I. Scene I. "The blessed little babes, God bless 'em!" Scene III. "Heaven be kind to us, for I've almost lost all other hope." Ditto. "Damn him." Scene IV. "Damn business." "No, don't damn business; I'm very drunk, but I can't damn business—it's profane." Ditto. "Isn't that an angel?" "I can't tell; I've not been used to such company." Scene V. "Oh, Martin, husband, for the love of heaven!" Ditto. "Heaven help us, heaven help us!" Act. II. Scene III. "Heaven forgive you, can you speak of it?" "I

leave you, and may heaven pardon and protect you!" Scene last.
"Farmer, neighbours, heaven bless you—let the landlord take all the
rest." Ditto. "They have now the money, and heaven prosper it with
them." [3]

Nevertheless, all the phrases that Colman deleted from the acting
version of the play were allowed to remain in subsequent published editions.

In true melodramatic fashion, Jerrold tells the story of Martin
Heywood, a poor farmer, who, along with his wife Rachel and
their five children, is faced with eviction from his farm. While the
absentee landlord, Grantley, spends his money at London gambling tables, the villain Crumbs, his dishonest steward, mercilessly
turns out tenants in order to profit from the auction of their possessions. The plot centers around the desperate Heywood family
and their futile attempts to gather payment of the rent. A stock
character of the pure and faithful wife, Rachel Heywood resists
the vile attempts of a scoundrel who tempts her virtue with
money. Just when the situation seems utterly hopeless for the
Heywoods, a small fortune is discovered in the chair of Martin's
grandfather.

In the subplot, two interlopers threaten to expose Crumbs as an
escaped prisoner. Meanwhile, pretending to be a London dandy
who is a friend of the master, Grantley has returned home. The
strangers arrange to rob him but are thwarted by Rachel, who
overhears their plans and warns Grantley. Thankful for his safety,
he awards the Heywoods a freeholder's rights to the farm, apolo-
gizes for his past irresponsibility, and reprimands Crumbs for his
dishonesty. Unlike the conventional villain of the melodrama,
Crumbs emerges as a partially sympathetic character when his
revenge upon his employer is explained by the fact that Grantley's
libertine father had years ago stolen his wife away from him.

Most of the other characters, however, are stock types. Similarly, the theme of the play, which pits the stonehearted landlord
against the pitiful family, was already a stock-in-trade among the
dramatists of the day. Although the play implies social criticism of
absentee landlords, the problem is never seriously treated. In fact,
it is never explained why young Grantley suddenly decides to return to London to check upon his servant, nor what prompts his
abrupt change from a gambler to a responsible landlord. Jerrold

primarily intended to reflect the hopes raised by the recent passage of the Reform Bill that justice and generosity would soon be granted to the poor.

Jerrold's next two plays exhibited a caustic satire and social consciousness not seen in his early works. *The Golden Calf* (1832) was aimed at the gross materialism of the day and ridiculed the sacrifices made to maintain appearances. *The Factory Girl* (1832) pleads the cause of the poor and oppressed class of society, a theme which dominated Jerrold's journalism and novels. The play depicts the horrors of a weaver's victimization in a factory where inhuman working conditions prevail.

In the story of *Nell Gwynne; or, the Prologue* (1833) Jerrold returns to the days of merry old England to tell of King Charles's notorious encounters with Nell, the "Orange Moll" of Drury Lane. The strength of the piece lies in the witty dialogue between Nell and her disguised suitor. Despite the prudery of a Covent Garden audience, Jerrold succeeded in making a heroine of England's most notorious whore. He accomplished this feat by adopting a naturalistic point of view. In a preface to the play, he explains his approach to the delicate subject: "The life of Nell Gwynne, from the time of her connexion with Charles the Second, to that of her death, proved that error had been forced upon her by circumstances, rather than indulged from choice. It was under this impression that the present little Comedy was undertaken. . . ." [4]

Produced the same year, *The Housekeeper* dealt with a conspiracy in the year 1772 to establish the Pretender on the throne. Working within another eighteenth-century setting, Jerrold attempted a comedy of manners with *Beau Nash, the King of Bath* (1834). Although there are some excellent duels of wit in this play, little attention is given to the strict rules of decorum which regulate the love affairs of traditional comedies of manner. Jerrold then toyed with the daring theme of marital infidelity in *The Mother* (1838), but any anxiety the audience suffered was allayed in the final act in which it is revealed that the supposed bastard was originally stolen from legitimate parents by a band of Gypsies.

IV The Prisoner of War *and* Bubbles of the Day

Despite Jerrold's active schedule with *Punch* and other journalism, he wrote eight plays between 1842 and 1854. During a visit to

Boulogne, he was preparing a comedy with the Englishman in France as its theme. When the peace of Amiens was broken by England within a year of its being made and the British minister left Paris, Napoleon retaliated by detaining all the British subjects who were in France. *The Prisoner of War* (1842) is concerned with a group of such Englishmen kept at Verdun. The self-satisfied patriot Pallmall and his vivacious sister Polly, believing the peace still intact, had come to France to improve their knowledge of the language. The comedy unfolds a sentimental story of love and combines with it the adventurous attempt of several Englishmen to escape from a prison fortress. Played to an audience with a strong national prejudice and an innate distrust of the French, this work had an especial appeal in the character of Pallmall, who can not only top the greatest boast of the French about their country's superiority but is made to spoof the excessive patriotism of the Englishman abroad who compulsively compares foreign customs unfavorably with his own. For example, after Pallmall is separated from his sister and sent to prison, he writes to her that he is teaching a spider to dance but "finds the spiders here nothing to the spiders in our summerhouse at Hornsey." He boasts that nightingales sing from every lamp in London and that he never saw a fog until he came to France.

The scene in which the Englishmen plot and effect their escape from the fortress also gains its humor at the expense of the English. After much careful planning, the prisoners dig a tunnel under the wall of the fortress. The moment of escape arrives, and all the inmates—after singing "Rule Britannia! Britannia, rule the waves! For Britons never, never shall be slaves"—begin their move to freedom, only to rush into a troop of French soldiers, who, informed of the escape, are patiently waiting to recapture their prisoners. Following the precepts of the melodrama, Jerrold resolves all the problems by having the governor of Verdun send a letter informing the English prisoners that they are to be exchanged for Frenchmen. The villain who reported the escape is punished by being sent to the dread fortress of Biche, and all the lovers are reunited.

Jerrold's awareness of the foolishness of melodrama is apparent in his parody of both the popular novel of romance and the sentimental love story in the subplot of his own *The Prisoner of War*. Afraid of her father's wrath, Clarina has kept her marriage a secret and continues to live at home. In an attempt to discern his reaction to her rash behavior, she reveals her plight to her father under the guise of a plot from a novel she has been reading:

Clar. It is a sad one. —The heroine is most unhappy.
Chan. That's usual.
Clar. For she has been disobedient.
Chan. That's nothing; for her father's a tyrant, a brute of course:
Clar. The best, the noblest, kindest parent!
Chan. Come, that's civil of the writer; he's not often so considerate. Fathers in novels are generally dragons in white wigs. Well, the girl?
Char. She is married.
Chan. What! unknown to her father, and he you say so kind, so good?
Clar. Her lover was her father's friend, his youthful friend, loved, assisted by him.
Chan. And the young gentleman, out of pure gratitude, makes a tool of the daughter—the scoundrel! How was the girl smitten? As they kill partridges, at first sight?
Clar. The lover was invited to her father's house. When his duties called him thence, 'twas then she felt the ties that bound her; 'twas then she felt the sweet and bitter grief of early love—of love nurtured in secret and deceit. In one passionate moment, forgetful of her duty as a daughter, heedless of him, whose every glance was affection, whose every word was doting, she cast away the memories of her childhood, the gratitude, the respect of youth, and became a wife—a wretched wife.
Chan. So! the villain who betrayed her duty, turned her tyrant?
Clar. No; for years she never saw him; from the day she called him husband.
Chan. Why then wretched?
Clar. She still dwelt with her father. The sense of her hyprocrisy, like a lingering poison, wore her; and the daily blessing of her father, that should have fallen like balm upon her, self-reproach did turn to blighting and a curse.
Chan. Poor thing! but she deserved to suffer. Well, and the husband? He returned?
Clar. He did.
Chan. And the father of his own sagacity discovered the match!
Clar. Once—they were together—such discovery was nearly made.
Chan. Ha! and the end of the story?
Clar. The end? It is not yet accomplished.
Chan. Yes, I see; there you turned down the page when I interrupted you. But I can tell the end of it. Oh, yes, the young couple go

upon their knees, the father swears a little, then takes out his pocket handkerchief, wipes his eyes, and forgives them.

Clar. Is such the ending? dear father, can you promise it?

Chan. To be sure I can, as well as if I had written it. Don't all novels end so? But if I were the father—[5]

Clarina, the typical ingenue of the melodrama, like the weeping heroines of countless romances, does indeed receive the expected forgiveness and a promise of lifelong marital bliss. After exposing the absurdity of the melodramatic convention, Jerrold turns around and exploits its full pathetic potential in the final scene. Not many dramatists at this time were willing to run the risks involved in satirizing their own stock-in-trade.

Jerrold's farcical comedy *Bubbles of the Day* (1842) abounds with caricatures of contemporary types that delighted audiences at Covent Garden and carried the play for a successful run. Lord Skindeep, member of Parliament for Muffborough, is the self-seeking aristocrat who makes an ostentatious show of philanthropy. He is contrasted with Chatham Brown, a member of the House of Commons, also for Muffborough, who prefers pursuing women to a career in statesmanship. Skindeep's butler, Corks, is a young radical who takes delight in secretly attacking his master's hypocrisy in the weekly newspapers under the pseudonym of Brutus the Elder.

City shams are represented by the alderman, Sir Phenix Clearcake, who is arranging a bazaar to gather funds to restore respectability to St. Paul's by having it painted. Captain Smoke, a veteran of the Madagascar Fusileers who relinquished his army career to enter commerce and improve mankind, represents the speculator. One of his many projects is to form a company to lease Mount Vesuvius for the manufacture of lucifer matches. Melon, a young barrister in the clutches of usurer Malmsey Shark, is faced with marrying a woman who will bring him money but not love.

The plot evolves from Melon's dilemma. His father and Mr. Spreadweasel, an Horatio Alger figure, arranged for the marriage of Melon to Pamela Spreadweasel. According to the terms of the will left by his father, Melon must marry Pamela or forfeit his fortune to her. If she marries another man first, the money goes to Melon. Since they both love someone else, they plan how to make the other marry first; and most of the other characters are quickly drawn into the plotting. Although Florentia, Pamela's confidante, is pursued by Sir Phenix, she winds up after numerous intrigues as Melon's wife. But the marriage occurs only after Pamela gratuitously forfeits the Melon inheritance and marries Chatham Brown, whereby she avoids Lord Skindeep, her father's choice for her husband.

The last scene abounds in revelations and reformations. Not only are all the love matches settled and Corks exposed as Brutus the Elder, but it is also revealed that Captain Smoke is actually Lord Skindeep's illegitimate son—a revelation that must have had a shocking effect upon audiences not accustomed to bastardy upon the stage. Convention is additionally outraged when Lord Skindeep is not punished for his early escapade, even though his desertion of the woman helped to bring about her death. He does, however, reform in the last scene—a reformation signaled by his open acknowledgement of his son and by his realization that the "human heart has chords." Chatham Brown also reforms by resigning from Parliament in order to undertake worthier duties.

Jerrold uses the time-worn device of the aside in this play for a new purpose. The technique serves not only to develop and to elucidate a plot filled with misapprehensions and complicated intrigues but to reflect the dual nature of all the characters. The whole world of the play is one fantastic deceit: Skindeep pretends to be philanthropic while he is actually self-seeking; Corks plays the role of the loyal butler, although he is attacking his master under an assumed name; Sir Phenix insists upon respectability but attempts to seduce one of Skindeep's teenaged servants; Captain Smoke cheats Spreadweasel out of money to raise bond to release Melon from prison; Florentia deceives Sir Phenix and marries Melon; Pamela pretends love for Skindeep and marries Chatham; Chatham acts out the part of a member of Parliament but his chief interest lies in wenching. Mainly through the use of asides, over one hundred and sixty of them, the author informs the audience of the characters' true thoughts and feelings; these comments function as a kind of masked comic chorus for the "open" dialogue of the play. Jerrold's experimental use of the aside may well have pointed the way to Eugene O'Neill's *Strange Interlude.*

V Time Works Wonders *and the Later Plays*

Time Works Wonders (1845) was met with enthusiastic applause from an audience that included nearly all the literary men of London. It ran for almost ninety nights to a full house and featured such well-known performers as Buckstone in the role of Bantam, Charles Matthews as Felix Goldthumb, and Madame Vestris (Mrs. Charles Matthews) as Bessy Tulip.

Originally called *School-Girl Love,* this comedy tells the story of a baronet's nephew who falls in love with a schoolgirl named Florentine, a baker's daughter. In an attempt to preserve the family dignity, Sir Gilbert severs the match by sending his nephew on a five-year tour of the Continent. In the interval, he himself meets Florentine and falls in love with her, not knowing she is the lowly baker's daughter. By the end of the play, however, Sir Gilbert realizes that love cannot be bound by social caste, subdues his pride, and blesses the marriage of Clarence and Florentine.

The plot has its counterpart in another love match that is also forbidden by paternal pride. Like Clarence, Felix Goldthumb has been sent away by his father in the hope that travel will check his supposed immorality in London. Unknown to his father, he returns with a new bride, Bessy Tulip, the girl who five years earlier had helped Florentine escape from boarding school to marry Clarence. Although Mr. Goldthumb, an ex-trunk-maker who recently inherited considerable property, has the severe mind of a stoic, he is easily won over by his son's affections and accepts Bessy as his daughter.

In still a third plot, there is the love affair between old Professor Truffles, a wandering scholar who travels with the solar system in a deal box, and Miss Tucker, the proud, self-righteous, and sentimental head of a girls' boarding school that has been ruined by Florentine's and Bessy's escape with Clarence. As in the other two plots, there is a *volte-face* when the genial, pompous professor intends "to mary, and—scholastically—have girls and boys."

The strength of the play lies in the well-handled action of the opening scenes and in the characters of Professor Truffles, Miss Tucker, and Goldthumb. The drama comes to life when Florentine and Bessy, fleeing with Clarence from Miss Tucker's boarding school, enter a country inn where Felix and Professor Truffles are dining. Just as the half-starved girls are about to feast on their eggs and bacon, Miss Tucker appears at the door and orders them bound hand and foot. They are pursued, captured, and sent back to school—but not before Miss Tucker discovers Professor Truffles' presence and with renewed hope recalls her abiding affection for him. The exposition exhibits a marked development in the structure of farce: it evolves naturally from the hurly-burly of the initial action, introduces all the major characters, and establishes two of the three love plots.

Dickens, who believed *Time Works Wonders* to be the best of Jerrold's plays, explained its appeal to him: "I am greatly struck by the whole idea of the piece. The elopement in the beginning, and the consequences that flow from it, and their delicate and masterly exposition, are the freshest, truest, and most vigorous kind; and the wit and wisdom of it are never asunder." [6]

The scene of *The Catspaw* (1850) is set in the very year of its initial appearance. A nobleman has died; and Snowball, the man who had hoped to inherit his fortune, insists that the will be handled through Chancery. His insistence is only in the way of friendliness, however, for, if the case is likely to go against him, he wishes to make it possible to marry the widow Peachdown, to whom the wealth has been left. He is made the "catspaw" by several people, notably by a quack medical attendant named Petgoose and by the resourceful widow. Jerrold's Doctor Petgoose anticipates by some years Richard Feverel's father (in George Meredith's *The Ordeal of Richard Feverel*) citing epigrams from his book, *Pilgrim's Scrip*. Petgoose, quoting from his volume, *Pearls to Pigs*, instructs the other characters that "not to blush for poverty is to want a proper respect for wealth"; that "human happiness is a plant that, when it will not grow of itself, may be forced to grow"; and that "the daisy is death's forget-me-not." [7]

The widow Peachdown won the affection of the audience with her ruling passion for the Middle Ages: "Why did I live in this drowsy, afternoon time of the world? Why not in the roseate dawn of chivalry, when my own true knight—knights might be had for love, and not money then—would have carried off my cause upon his lance, and me upon his palfrey afterwards!" [8] Her proudest possession is a scale model of Stonehenge, which serves as her work table. After numerous intrigues, involving romantic subplots, Mrs. Peachdown wins Snowball for her husband and plans a solemn bridal procession consisting of archers from Drury Lane, crossbowmen from the Opera House, falconers from the Zoological Gardens, a dwarf, a fool, and other representatives of the good old times.

Retired from Business (1851) satirizes contemporary social

climbing and pretense. The scene is laid in Pumpkinfield, a paradise for retired tradesmen and merchants who desire to hide the
taint of their middle-class backgrounds under the façade of their
villas and fine coaches. The plot revolves around the comic attempts of Mr. and Mrs. Pennyweight to adjust to this "golden
fringe of existence." Mr. Pennyweight is a candid man who is not
ashamed of the greengrocer's shop from which he has come; his
wife, in contrast, devotes herself to imitating the absurdities of her
new environment. After Puffins, a Russian merchant, advises her
that in Pumpkinfield there is an impassable gulf between the gen-
try of wholesalers (the billocracy) and the vulgar retailers (the
tillocracy), Mrs. Pennyweight prefixes "Fitz" to their name, buys a
coat of arms, and lets it be thought that her husband is a merchant.

Love, however, cannot be bound by caste; and young Paul
Puffins, "a child of nature," falls in love with Kitty Pennyweight.
When Mr. Pennyweight's true past as a shopkeeper is revealed,
his neighbors forgive him, and the play ends on a happy note with
some moralizing about society's "false distinctions, made by ignorance, maintained by weakness." Although Mr. Pennyweight coop-
erates with his wife's earnest game of pretense, he preserves his
essential humanity throughout the play; and he serves as Jerrold's
satiric commentator upon the quest for respectability, the social
blight of the rising middle class. Similarly, Paul's marriage to Kitty
is meant as an object lesson that human nature cannot be subju-
gated to social and economic status.

Two years passed before the production of Jerrold's next play,
St. Cupid; or, Dorothy's Fortune, which was given a command
performance at Windsor Castle. Curiously, Jerrold was not invited
to attend. Although several audiences were graciously extended to
the American showman Phineas T. Barnum and his protégé Tom
Thumb, most English authors were not yet considered respectable
enough to merit an invitation to Windsor Castle or to Buckingham Palace. Jerrold's frequent ridicule of Victoria and Albert in
Punch probably contributed to his unpopularity among the royal
family.

Jerrold's last play, *A Heart of Gold* (1854), is a farcical romance that tells the story of a girl named Maude who is wooed by
a wealthy old man and by a penniless youth. Dymond, the aged
suitor, dies and leaves his fortune to young Pierce Thanet, whom
he does not know to be his rival, with the stipulation that he never

relinquish the inheritance. It turns out, however, that Dymond was only in a cataleptic trance and after three days was restored to life. When Pierce keeps his promise and refuses to return the money to Dymond, Maude thinks he is greedy and refuses to marry him. Love finally overcomes conscience and Pierce restores the fortune to win Maude as his bride.

The play contained enough dramatic incidents, witty dialogue, and lively humor to sustain a successful performance, but it was miscast and poorly acted. The failure of the play, combined with a grievance with Charles Kean, led Jerrold to abandon the theater after a lifelong devotion that had made him one of the most popular dramatists of the century.

Compared to dramatists like Arthur Wing Pinero and George Bernard Shaw, Jerrold seems very mediocre indeed. However, Jerrold's dramatic ambitions were never grand. As an author of melodramas and farces, he was extremely skillful and successful. Although it is now fashionable to sneer at Victorian drama, its chief contribution to English and American culture—the melodrama—makes up the bulk of today's entertainment in motion pictures and on television. It must not be forgotten that the magic of the theater and the ability of a great actor could transmute a mediocre script into an exciting evening's entertainment. Jerrold's plays brought tears and laughter not only from uneducated masses but from men of no less cultivated taste than Charles Dickens.

The plays of Thomas William Robertson, Shaw, Henry Arthur Jones, and Pinero grew directly out of the kind of drama in which Jerrold excelled. These were the plays they were seeing as children; later they would learn by reacting against them and by making their plays more natural, reflective, and problematic. Still, Jerrold's efforts to restore a native English drama that depended upon its dialogue rather than its machinery remain an important link in the evolution of the drama.

Popular taste, meanwhile, has swung full circle. Considering that the present generation has enshrined soap operas and situation comedy, one would think Jerrold's plays would have an enormous appeal today. After all, there is not much difference between James Bond and his force of aquamen destroying the enemy and Lieutenant Pike and his troop of marines capturing the smugglers.

CHAPTER 3

The World of Punch

I *The Spirit of the Jester*

ALTHOUGH some literary historians have credited Jerrold with either founding or editing *Punch*, according to Thackeray he did neither;[1] in fact, during the time the staff was forming and preparing its first number, Jerrold was with his family in Boulogne. The newly established staff wrote asking him to join as a contributor for the first issue, but his essay, which arrived too late for the first number, appeared in the second. His opening paper, which was a satiric account of Peel's frustrations in the Bedchamber Crisis, marked the beginning of Jerrold's lifelong association with *Punch*.

Before he joined the magazine, Jerrold was primarily known as a successful playwright, having by 1841 written over fifty plays. In his new career, he was to become notorious as the gadfly of the aristocracy, the High Church, the royal family, political conservatives, and even of P. T. Barnum. His sixty-five political leaders signed "Q" became extremely popular and were chiefly responsible for establishing the radical tone of the journal. M. F. Spielmann, the historian of *Punch*, considers Jerrold "the man to whom, more than anyone else, the paper owed the enormous political influence it once enjoyed, and to whom it is indebted for much of the literary reputation it still retains. . . ."[2] By 1845, when Mrs. Job Caudle made her vociferous debut in *Mrs. Caudle's Curtain Lectures*, Jerrold had become the undisputed claimant for the title of "Mr. Punch." Not even Thackeray was able to surpass the success of that popular serial.

Punch was produced by a small staff that was in constant argument and convivality, and unity in its point of view and spirit may be traced to this fact. The entire contents, letterpress and cartoons, were discussed by the whole staff. Like the *New Yorker*,

Punch was established by collecting, training, and supporting a group of writers on whom the paper could rely and who were subject to a minimum of editorial direction. Writers were paid a weekly salary and had a certain number of allotted columns to fill. Jerrold, the highest-paid contributor, received two pounds a week; the others, only one pound a week each. Despite the anonymity of articles in *Punch,* the magazine's circulation still depended upon the star system, established mainly by the great popularity of Jerrold's and Thackeray's serials. Sometimes the authorship leaked out, and occasionally a writer signed his work with a characteristic mark such as Jerrold's famous "Q." Neither Jerrold nor Thackeray favored the policy of anonymity, for each felt it exalted the paper at the expense of the writers. But the editorial policy remained until recent years that there is only one *Punch* editor and his contributors are but the working parts of his body.

During the first few months of the new venture, the staff held its meetings in various taverns, especially the Crown Inn, Vinegar Yard; but after the magazine was acquired by the publishing firm of Bradbury and Evans, the discussions were moved to the *Punch* office. Every Wednesday evening members of the staff gathered around the table for dinner to consider the material for the next number. Here Jerrold was in his glory, showing off his sparkling wit, and setting the table in a roar of laughter. The story is told that when Thackeray once came late for a Wednesday meeting after being detained at a christening at which he had stood sponsor to his friend's boy, he was met with Jerrold's exclamation: "Good Lord, Thackeray! I hope you didn't present the child with your own mug!" And, when James Stirling asked what Thackeray was like, Jerrold replied: "He's just a big fellow with a broken nose, and, though I meet him weekly at the *Punch* dinner, I don't know him so well as I know you."

Thackeray did not like Jerrold's habit of monopolizing the conversation at the *Punch* table, where he was not only the readiest but the loudest talker. Sides soon were chosen, and there were frequent clashes between the gentlemanly and Bohemian standards: John Leech and Thackeray against Mark Lemon and Jerrold. Because Jerrold ate peas with a knife, Thackeray did not consider him fit company. And Leech, also distressed by Jerrold's

"low breeding," used to imitate him at Rose Cottage by throwing
his hair back and sprinkling salt with gusto over his gooseberry
tart.[3]

Such differences gradually led to a duel for supremacy between
Jerrold and Thackeray. One of their contemporaries has stated
that Jerrold was "the one literary man of whom Thackeray, when
in his prime, seemed to be seriously jealous." [4] Upon receiving a
newly delivered *Punch*, Thackeray would tear off the wrapper to
see what "Master Douglas" has to say this week. Through 1845,
the year *Mrs. Caudle's Curtain Lectures* secured both its creator
and *Punch* their greatest fame and fortune, Jerrold was virtually
unrivaled. In the next year, however, Thackeray's *The Snobs of
England* won for him the crown of Mr. Punch, and the whole
emphasis of the magazine shifted permanently from the broadly
comic to the urbane.

The unmeasured buffoonery and the radical view of politics
and society that lay at the heart of *Punch's* early success were
never congenial to Thackeray. Lacking the personal experience of
poverty, which had ingrained in Jerrold the convictions that the
"Condition-of-England Question," as Thomas Carlyle called it,
was of such great importance as to overshadow all other matters,
Thackeray had never indulged in the attacks upon property and
in the threats to constituted authority which were essential items
of Jerrold's stock-in-trade. The exclusive humanitarianism in Jerrold's point of view was foreign to Thackeray's nature; for, in
comparing the two men, Gordon Ray has written that, "anything
but a revolutionary, he [Thackeray] became conscious through
his opposition to Jerrold of his true role as a writer, to describe
with wit, urbanity, and healthy feeling the life that he knew best,
the life of middle- and upper-class England." [5]

Thackeray once came to the point of resigning from *Punch* because of an "incendiary article" Jerrold proposed to publish; but it
was either withdrawn or modified, for Thackeray continued to
contribute to the magazine. In his first paper "On Clerical Snobs"
Thackeray reproved those journalists who constantly satirize the
clergy, and he argued that most Victorian parsons lived good
lives. Jerrold, who took this statement about the clergy to be a
direct reproof of himself, moderated his anticlericalism. Thackeray commented upon his victory: "Two years ago I used only to
make a passive opposition agst [*sic*] the Anti-church and Bishop

sneers—last year I made an active one (Jerrold and I had a sort of
war and I came off conqueror). . . ." [6] It is little wonder, then,
that Thackeray, who used to sit at Jerrold's side at the *Punch* din-
ners, changed his seat in order to face his best of enemies across
the table.

It is a remarkable tribute to *Punch's* comic ingenuity and good
taste that it could for so many years consistently provide entertainment without resorting to vulgar or sexual subjects. Because it
aimed at a family audience, *Punch* allowed the Victorian father to
bring it home without any shame. Indeed, the *Somerset County
Gazette* called it "the first comic we ever saw which was not vulgar. It will provoke many a hearty laugh, but never call a blush to
the most delicate cheek." [7] And Thackeray wrote to Mr. Punch:
"We will laugh in the company of our wives and children; we will
tolerate no indecorum; we like that our matrons and girls should
be pure." [8]

As a general statement it is perfectly true that *Punch's* respectability increased its potential public more and more as Regency
England became Victorianized; but isolated examples of vulgarity
and sexuality can be found in *Punch,* written notably by Jerrold.
This vulgar streak in his humor, however, seems mild when compared to the standards of the great humorists throughout the cen-
turies. There are indecorous allusions to the posterior of one's
anatomy by which Jerrold hoped to shock the refined sensibilities
of the prudish middle class. Even in the popular *Mrs. Caudle's
Curtain Lectures* there is a suggestion of marital infidelity in Job
Caudle's solicitous behavior toward Miss Prettyman. Perhaps
most surprising, however, is the almost boundless freedom allowed Jerrold and others to attack the royal family and the government leaders. Whereas the government censored the *damns*
out of his plays, it permitted Jerrold to caricature Prince Albert as
an impractical, foolhardy factotum who was more concerned with
designing Hessian hats and in keeping the royal bees than he was
with the welfare of his country.

II *"Prime Minister of Punch"*

It is surprising that Mark Lemon all but omitted the subject
of politics from his discussion of "The Moral of Punch" in the first
number of the magazine. He only says that "party *must* destroy
patriotism." [9] It was not until two years later that Jerrold made

Punch's political point of view explicit when, writing as Mr. Punch, candidate for Parliament from London, he stated the magazine's platform: "As for my politics, men of London, they are of all sides, and all parties: hence, Tory, Whig, Conservative, and Radical, may with perfect consistency give me their vote: for as the pine-apple—as my friend Moon says—combines in itself a smack, a relish of every other fruit, so do I possess a shade and hue of every party under the sun." [10] The ideal was to strike at any group when the occasion demanded it; but more accurately, in practice, *Punch* leaned toward a moderate liberalism in sympathy with the poor and oppressed and with the popular cause of freedom. In his Edinburgh speech of 1893, Gladstone said: "There is a popular periodical which, whenever it can, manifests the Liberal sentiments by which it has been guided from the first. I mean the periodical Punch." [11]

The liberal tradition of the magazine may be traced to Jerrold's political essays that began to appear in the second number and continued until his death. The first few years were particularly crucial in forming the political character of *Punch,* and it was then that Jerrold was writing his most outspoken radical papers over the signature "Q." Jerrold, like Mr. Punch, was neither a Whig nor a Conservative; his political beliefs were those of a radical democrat. He believed in sweeping changes in legislation and in governmental practices brought about by due process of law, not by revolution. Although he championed the progressive demands of the Chartist Movement, he withdrew his support when its leaders resorted to physical violence.

Jerrold's democratic principles provide the point of view of almost every political essay he ever wrote. He believed in a representative democracy in which the needs of the populace would be justly represented in Parliament by representatives with a sincere concern for their constituencies. But the middle and the upper classes did not figure in his concept of democracy; he thought of the populace as consisting only of the poor and oppressed. His sympathy with the workers of Bolton and Manchester, for the beggars of London, and for the weavers at Paisley led him to make violent attacks upon private property and authority. His distrust of authority began with his youthful experiences in the navy when he had witnessed the horrors of war and had observed how authority had had to be enforced by flogging.

Because Jerrold ruled the political roost of the publication, he was christened by the historian of *Punch* as *"Punch's* Prime Minister." As such, he immediately came into conflict with the conservatism of Sir Robert Peel. As a champion of the poor, Jerrold wanted reform in the Corn Laws and in the Income Tax, and he repeatedly attacked Peel for making too little progress toward alleviating the poverty of the lower classes. Indeed, Jerrold's democratic principles were at the bottom of his lifelong crusade against the aristocracy. He was so fiercely upright and aggressive that his impulsiveness often blinded him and led him to make irrational accusations against the rich. But he was never a demagogue: not even his most hostile critics ever accused him of making capital of popular discontent for selfish motives. He sincerely thought that England's aristocrats had an enormous responsibility to the poor that they were shamefully abusing, and he felt it his duty as a journalist and as a humanitarian to arouse public opinion against the injustice.

English royalty also conflicted with Jerrold's political bias. He viewed the royal family as an expensive museum piece burdening the English economy. He portrays Victoria as a mere puppet mouthing the speeches of Peel and Albert as an ineffectual factotum lacking rapport with the common man. Yet despite his antiroyalist prejudice, Jerrold sympathized with Victoria for being politically dominated by Peel; and he turned his satire away from politics to royalty's social functions, such as their visits to Scotland and patronage of the arts. Even though Queen Victoria insisted that she was no mere child during the Bedchamber Question in 1839, Peel appears to have taken full control of the political situation soon after. Jerrold pictures the Queen as "Peel's Victim" in 1844: "Ere *Punch* shall have issued his next sheet, her Gracious Majesty will have enacted a part of *Juliet* before the mob of Parliament. She speaks; yet she says nothing. Dear lady! Deeply, indeed, shall we sympathize with her, drawn to the House, with nothing better than Sir Robert Peel's words in her mouth for public delivery." [12] The essay constitutes an attack upon the empty spectacle of royalty. Jerrold first creates a vivid picture of the royal procession to Parliament in order to contrast it with the Prime Minister's "shabby message." The procession is presented from two opposing points of view: first, through an analysis of the crowd's reaction, and then directly through the eyes of Mr. Punch. Jack Nokes,

one of the crowd, is caught up in the colorful spectacle: "Jack
Nokes has, for a second, a vague notion that he is a bit of the
monarchy; that the show is a part of his property; that the Life
Guards and the state coaches, and the Lord Chamberlain and
the Ladies of the Bedchamber, and more—that her Gracious Majesty herself—are, at least a portion of them, his goods." Then Mr.
Punch, who has given the procession more careful thought, states
his own perspective:

With very different feelings does *Punch* watch her Majesty's progress
to Parliament. There sits Victoria, framed and glazed, in that beautiful
coach, and looking happy, and throwing smiles about her, wide as the
sun; and there sits Prince Albert, contented as Jack Horner with his
finger on his plum. . . .
    And this spectacle, glorious as it is to thoughtless eyes, to the vision
of *Punch* is sad, yea, dolorous. The excess of his grief arises from the
superabundance of his loyalty. She has dressed herself, she and her
household too have prepared themselves,—she, her women and her
maids, her Life Guards, and her black cymbal-players, her horses,
her asses, and the rest of the ministry,—and all to deliver a shabby
message from Tamworth!

Jerrold then draws a comparison between the Queen's opening of
Parliament and disreputable Bob Slimely's "opening" of a tenement. Bob contrives a story to get into the tenement and has Victoria Windsor, "a frank-hearted female" of the village, repeat it to
the owner of the place. Once in, Bob steals "tariff beef" from the
larder and ransacks the whole house. Jerrold hopes that by this
comparison he has educated his readers to the political facts ob-
scured by pomp and circumstance: "Now, reader, we see it; you
melt with pity at the hard fate of Victoria Windsor, compelled by
Bob to say a string of nothings to Mrs. Stephens; and yet, such is
the ignorance of man! You bellow huzza! huzza! when her Gracious Majesty, with Peel's speech in her mouth, opens Parliament."
    This essay is followed by a two-page-width cartoon by Kenny
Meadows illustrating the procession, at the end of which is pictured an ass with the face of John Roebuck, a radical member of
Parliament, who neatly and unobtrusively figures in the parade in
the same way that Jerrold suggests the Queen's entourage included "her asses and the *rest* of her ministry." Jerrold's essay goes

beyond the cartoon in its suggestion that royalty's role in politics is confined to fancy coaches: Victoria is "framed and glazed" as an expensive museum piece. Jerrold reminds the reader that it costs seventy thousand pounds annually to maintain the royal stables when thousands of human beings are poverty stricken and starving. But, despite his antiroyalist sentiment, Jerrold reveals his sympathy for the Queen who must play her role as puppet to a politician. Even in the illustrative comparison he makes, she is referred to as a "frank-hearted female"; whereas Peel is compared to a burglar who takes advantage of her village simplicity.

Jerrold's satire of the royal family is essentially impersonal in that he considers its members in the role of a symbol representing England, rather than as individuals. He felt that royalty did not do justice to the living English artists and authors; although Victoria frequently attended the patent theaters, they were often performing foreign operas, plays, and musical events. After her fiftieth visit to the theater, Jerrold sarcastically praises her loyalty to the arts: "It is this devoted, we may say affectionate, solicitude of Her Majesty, towards the literature and arts of her own country that has secured to her the blessing of the Muses of England. From the top of her crown to the extreme point of her satin slipper, her Majesty is all English—and the English drama and English music her especial delights." [13]

The public often wondered what persuaded Queen Victoria and her husband to attend hunts. Some of the press disparaged these adventures, some simply reported them, and Jerrold was outrightly indignant about them. After the queen's attendance at an otter hunt at Blair Athol, Jerrold writes that the Society for the Prevention of Cruelty to Animals, which interfered with the poor man's cock fights and dog fights, should now feel itself rebuked by royal approval of cruelty to animals. But Jerrold was most upset over the deer-killing episode at Saxe-Gotha when Albert made a trip to his native country of Coburg and was drawn by his hosts into the sport of deer shooting *à la battue,* while Victoria looked on. After the queens and duchesses had entered the pavilion and the gentlemen had taken up their positions beside a table stacked with ammunition, beaters drove the deer into the enclosure, and the sportsmen covered the field with dead and wounded animals. In the intervals required for lesser huntsmen to slit the throats of the wounded deer, a military band played lively polkas and national airs. The carnage festival continued for two hours, and then the ladies departed through avenues of the dead animals. The event inspired a parody by Jerrold:

> Sing a song of Gotha—a pocket full of rye,
> Eight-and-forty timid deer driven in to die;
> When the sport was open'd, all bleeding they were seen—
> Wasn't that a dainty dish to set before a Queen?

> The Queen sat in her easy chair, and look'd as sweet as honey;
> The Prince was shooting at the deer, in weather bright and sunny;
> The bands were playing Polkas, dress'd in green and golden clothes;
> The Nobles cut the poor deer's throats, and that is all *Punch* knows.[14]

The contrast between the singsong innocence of the nursery rhyme and the gore of the event makes the parody particularly effective, and the choice of the well-known verse guarantees that all the readers will participate in its fun. The second couplet is the only one with a rhyme not found in the original poem, and the last rhyme, *knows,* humorously echoes the *nose* that was bitten off in the original version.

The Queen's travels always rated high interest in the eyes of the public. The press would cover royalty's slightest movement away from home for the edification of readers. When the Queen went to Scotland, Sir Andrew Agnew wrote a letter to the Earl of Aberdeen, intended as a sort of side-wind letter to the queen. It was meant as a lecture to her on keeping the sabbath in Scotland better than she had been keeping it in England. Jerrold, who had absolutely no sympathy with the Sabbatarians, satirizes Agnew's letter: "Thus, Sir Andrew hopes that, on the Sabbath, the Queen will encourage no quadrille parties; that Prince Albert will not whistle 'My Heart's in the Highlands'; and that the little Princess will especially not play at 'Beggaring my Neighbor' with Lady Caroline Cocks." [15]

Jerrold relies heavily upon wit and imagination in his political writings and is concerned with politics as a moralist, not as a pragmatist. He ridicules Peel's equivocation on the Corn Laws, not because he dislikes Peel or wants simply to amuse the readers of *Punch*, but because he believed these laws were keeping hungry people from cheap bread. This simple, almost naïve concept of right and wrong always characterizes Jerrold's politics. He is not concerned with the intricacies of political machinery or with the subtleties of legislation. He is, therefore, often unfair to his opponents, who, being human, cannot possibly measure up to the black and white categories of his moral and political creed.

James Hutchinson Stirling, the Scottish philosopher, said that on great questions of the day Jerrold felt out of his depth—that before he could speak he required some anecdote, some sally of general humanity, to give him a meaning and a purpose.[16] The truth of this observation may be seen in Jerrold's first few political papers. Instead of dealing with the new administration's policies or past record, he raises the old Bedchamber Question and brings Peel down to the domestic level of quarreling over a retinue of women for a teenage queen. Yet even under this ridicule lies Jerrold's moral judgment that Peel, by involving himself in such quibbling, is permitting the grave issues of the Corn Laws and of a just property tax to go by the board. This typical technique he employed throughout his political essays, and consequently one seldom obtains a direct account of such important issues as the Corn Laws, Chartism, or the Factory Act of 1848. James Hannay suggests that this indirection is due to Jerrold's being a humorist who fought with the weapons of a man of letters instead of those of a politician.[17] Also, as a journalist, not as a historian, he did not need to explain the current events that his readers knew all about from the newspapers.

Jerrold states that the purpose of his political essays is "to give brief suggestions for the better government of the world, and for bringing about the millennium. . . ."[18] Despite his earnestness in correcting and attacking the injustices of his time, his humorous perspective enabled him to view objectively his own efforts to make government more just. He had the good sense to realize that he was no John Locke or Thomas Hobbes, and he gladly settled for his role as comic interpreter of the political times, employing literary devices instead of political philosophy and statistics to defeat his foes.

Before his defeat in 1846, Sir Robert Peel had abolished the duties on 605 articles, and he had reduced the rate on most of those that remained dutiable. During these experiments in the direction of free trade, however, Peel maintained that the duties on sugar and corn required special treatment. In 1845 the Corn Law League had sent to Peel some velveteen for trousers, in which was secretly woven ears of wheat and the word *free*. When Peel discovered the sartorial symbolism, he returned the material and had his letter of refusal printed in *The Times*.[19] Jerrold, who spotted the absurd incident, extended the jest further: "Great, indeed, would have been the triumph of the League, if the Minister had donned the insidious trousers, and, taking his seat in them in the House of Commons, had, without knowing it, based his ministry upon—'free corn!' "[20] The vulgar streak in Jerrold's humor is well exemplified by his imaginative version of what would have happened if Peel, with dramatic irony, had worn the treacherous trousers.

Jerrold obviously expected his readers to remember this incident, because three years later, when Peel changed his position on the Corn Laws, he alluded to it again. He declares that times have changed and that now Peel would like "Free Corn" inscribed a thousand times upon his coat and waistcoat. He then prints a fictitious letter in which Peel asks that the velveteen be returned to him. This letter counterbalances the one Peel actually did write three years earlier and reminds the reader of his original rejection of the velveteen.

Jerrold's radical democratic beliefs were so consistent that one can readily predict his position on most topics. In his essays on Chartism, he is naturally on the side of the popular cry for reform. Daniel O'Connell, the Irish nationalist, is denounced as a demagogue for falsely representing the common man of Ireland. Sir James Graham, the home secretary, is severely attacked for interfering with the cause of liberty on the Continent by opening some of Giuseppe Mazzini's letters. Alderman Peter Laurie is persistently ridiculed for unfairly sentencing the destitute of London to prison. But Jerrold's attitude toward the political rights of the Jews is ambiguous: although supporting Jewish emancipation on the rational principle that the Jews have certain inalienable human rights, he nevertheless ridicules them as lazy money-lenders. Like Gilbert à Beckett and John Leech, he had an anti-Semitic streak. And Mark Lemon, who was part Jewish, did nothing to temper the flood of merciless derision that *Punch* for a while poured on the whole House of Israel.

The job of writing the Preface to a complete volume of *Punch*

often fell to Jerrold. For the 1844 volume, he conceived the idea
of inventing various prize prefaces sent into *Punch* by illustrious
men, such as the Duke of Wellington, Sir Robert Peel, Henry
Brougham, and Benjamin Disraeli.[21] Disraeli's "Prize Preface" ridicules his Judaism:

It has been remarked by the surpassing author of the brilliant *Coningsby,* that the world, although it dreams not of the glory, is at the
present time governed by the Hebrew mind! Punch can bear testimony
to the fact. Once Punch wanted money. Who lent it to him at sixty per
cent?—a Jew! Who sued him on the bill?—a Jew! Who arrested him?
—a Jew? Who sold him up?—a Jew! These however, are common
events. The world, however, will be startled to learn that Punch himself—witness his nose—is a Jew.[22]

By combining Disraeli's well-known belief in the historical mission of the Jews with the caricature of *Punch,* Jerrold achieves his
satiric effect. Disraeli had stated that Jesus and his followers were
all Jews, that the infallible throne of Rome was established by a
Jew, and that England would not be a Christian country if it had
not been for a Jew. Even in *Coningsby,* the powerful master
financier, Sidonia, is a Spanish-Moslem Jew. Jerrold pays satiric
tribute to the Hebrew mind that governs the world by imagining
Mr. Punch completely surrounded by Jews whose power lies in
their heartless, treacherous usury. And since Judaism appears to
be engulfing the world, Jerrold offers up Mr. Punch to Disraeli's
claim for Israel.

Because of his ambiguous attitude towards the Jews, Jerrold's
irony once returned upon himself. He had written an article in
Punch poking fun at the *Morning Post*'s use of the term "gentlemen Jews." He said that Jews have risen from being called "ac-
cursed dogs" to "individuals of the Jewish persuasion," to "persons
of the Hebrew faith," and now to "gentlemen Jews." Satirically,
Jerrold called for a reversion to the good old days when "good,
strong, stringent prejudices" were "intended to hold society together. . . ."[23] Some readers misunderstood this article, however,
taking it to be anti-Semitic. Complaints were written in to the
Times, the *Morning Chronicle,* and *Punch* itself. Jerrold then had
to direct an explanation to those offended: "In our sufferings,
however, we have illustrious company. Great men, even before
Punch, have been misunderstood and reviled by dulness for their

best intentions. One Daniel Defoe wrote *A Short Way with the Dissenters,* satirically advocating their social rights; when his leathern-eared clients read him backwards, and would have sacrificed their champion." [24]

III   Comic Diplomacy

Punch was so outspoken on foreign affairs that in 1843 it was banned in France. In the first half-volume of that year a cartoon entitled "Punch turned out of France"—showing a seasick puppet received on the Boulogne quay at the point of a bayonet—first made public the magazine's severe struggle with Louis Philippe. The cartoon refers the reader to page seventy-five, where Jerrold, one of the writers responsible for *Punch's* expulsion, explains "The Wrongs of Punch." The embargo was lifted about two months later, but in the following year an article by Thackeray entitled "A Case of Real Distress," in which *Punch* offers to open a subscription for the poor beggar, Philippe, caused a second expulsion of the magazine. No doubt the accompanying illustration by Thackeray representing the king as a "Pauvre Malheureux" hastened the censorship.

These incidents are a clear indication of the seriousness with which *Punch's* views about foreign affairs were received. Most of Jerrold's essays in this area were directed against France and Louis Philippe in particular; however, he also made sharp attacks upon America, the king of Hanover, and Czar Nicholas I. As a liberal democrat, he was vigorous in his support of Giuseppe Mazzini's struggles to free Italy from Austrian domination. His anti-royalist prejudices were not confined to his own country, but were behind his attacks upon foreign monarchs. The principles of equality and justice that led him to denounce the Game Laws and the Poor Laws were even more violently outraged by the bloodshed of innocent people by Nicholas in Poland and by Philippe in Algeria.

Jerrold's firm belief in the equality of people, in part supported by England's abolition of the slave trade early in the century, was behind his sarcastic denunciation of slavery in America. He also opposed America's imperialism in Mexico and its stand on the Oregon Question. On the same basis, he condemned the imperialism of France. Since Jerrold was not a rabid patriot, most of his writings are severely critical in analyzing the problems of his own country. In his comedy, *The Prisoner of War*, he even presents a satiric caricature of the English patriot in France that shows he possessed a genuine sense of humor about his own country and the foolish excesses of patriotism. Therefore, *Punch's* attacks upon foreign countries may be accepted as coming from one who has first sought to clean his own house.

Jerrold was given the job of accounting for *Punch's* expulsion from France, which he did in the form of a letter to the Citizen King from Mr. Punch recently returned from Boulogne where he was greeted by a bayonet.[25] In this manner, he connects his essay directly with the cartoon. He then relates a conversation between Mr. Punch and a Frenchman whom he met in Dover upon his return; and, through this dialogue, the reader learns the reasons behind Mr. Punch's expulsion. The Frenchman accuses him of calling Philippe hard names for his intrigues with Spain, of sneering at French colonies and at General Bugeaud, of desecrating the eloquence of Alexandre Dumas, of placing Napoleon on a monument of froth spouting imperial pop, and of questioning the right of France to wage war on others. Jerrold was soon to become guilty of all the charges except the one about Napoleon; but, in 1843, he was only culpable upon the first two accusations.

After Thackeray's essay had the magazine banned a second time, Jerrold wrote an article entitled "Wanted.—A Few Bold Smugglers!" in the style of the newspaper "want ad," in which he asks for smugglers to help *Punch* continue "to disseminate civilisation throughout benighted France" and to convert Frenchmen "from the false worship of blood and fire." [26] Jerrold began his most abusive attacks upon the French after this second embargo where, week after week, he attacked France for its brutality in Algiers. The Archbishop of Bordeaux, who praised the French soldiers for their bravery, was condemned as summarily as General Bugeaud for placing the sword before the cross. And, when Colonel Pelissier led French troops to destroy eight hundred men, women, and children, Jerrold again raised the theme of religious hypocrisy and declared the Colonel taught the infidels "the lovely meekness of the Christian faith." [27]

Czar Nicholas I of Russia was severely attacked by *Punch* for his brutal tyranny. Jerrold's liberal principles were outraged at every turn by Nicholas' ruthlessness. When the Emperor visited England in 1844, Jerrold wrote that the residents of Newgate were willing to illuminate the outside of the jail at their own expense "with the touching word—'Welcome!' " [28] He hated Nicholas for stripping the Polish of almost all national distinctions, for repressing all free thought in Russia, and for championing reaction throughout Europe. But Jerrold's special wrath was directed against his old enemy, the English aristocracy, for having so cordially received Nicholas into their circles: "Though steeped from head to heel in the blood and tears of Poland, he was approached as almost something divine by the aristocracy of England." [29] He condemns "those high-born ladies who thronged and fluttered about the man" even though he had murdered forty-seven Polish Catholic nuns near Minsk and ordered one hundred and fifty thousand Jews to the deserts of the interior of Russia. When the Pope and the Romans snubbed the Czar, Jerrold said "they showed higher morality than many of the English aristocracy," [30] which is a great concession from anti-Catholic Jerrold.

Jerrold's basic approach throughout these numerous short articles is to enumerate Nicholas' heinous crimes against humanity and then to revert to the warm reception he received from the aristocracy on his visit to England. Devoid of humor, the papers caricature Nicholas as a repulsive monster thriving on innocent blood. His death was immortalized in *Punch* by Leech's famous cartoon, "General Fevrier Turned Traitor," in which Fevrier appears as Death beckoning the Czar to follow him.

Jerrold, who saw many of his liberal democratic ideals actually carried out by Mazzini, was very much concerned in the 1840's over the uncertain fate of European freedom. In 1849 he wrote to his friend Mrs. Cowden Clarke of his disappointment over the collapse of the liberal movement on the Continent: "Mazzini, I hear, will be with us in a fortnight. European liberty is, I fear, manacled and gagged for many years." [31] Jerrold's sympathy with Mazzini's cause brought the following undated letter by Mazzini to him: "I know that you would not fail me if everybody did. . . . But I know more; and it is that, whenever you do sympathize, you are ready to act, to embody your feelings in good, visible, tangible symbol; and this is not the general rule." [32]

In 1853, Jerrold presented, as has been earlier observed, a souvenir of the works of Shakespeare to the famous Hungarian patriot, Louis Kossuth; and his presentation speech is a clear example of what Mazzini had written about in his letter. Jerrold praises Kossuth for his struggle against the Austrians and expresses the hope that "the darkness that now benights the greater part of Continental Europe will be rolled away, dispersed by the light of liberty, like some suffocating fog." [33] Three years earlier, when Jerrold attempted to visit Austrian-dominated Italy, he had been refused entry into that country because of his liberal views.

Since England had abolished slavery early in the century, Jerrold could more righteously condemn America's treatment of the Negro without fear of rebuttal. It is hypocrisy, however, more than slavery, that he attacks: "The eagle steals its prey—America steals her blacks. The eagle will feed upon human flesh—so does America; that is, if the flesh have within it negro blood. The eagle —that is, the free American eagle—lays putrid eggs; nought wholesome, nought vital is produced from them." [34]

When President Tyler's life was saved by a Negro who arrested his runaway horses, Jerrold sarcastically expressed doubt that he could congratulate the President on the escape, "seeing that it makes him a debtor for his life to a black—a mere human chattel —a thing of sale and barter." [35] Jerrold, not satisfied with basing his sarcasm upon actual occurrences, declares that the Bible on which James Polk took the presidential oath "was very handsomely bound for the purpose in the skin of a negro." [36] The short articles against American slavery are many, but the theme is always hypocrisy. No attempt is made to analyze the problem of the American Negro: his condition is simply contrasted with the American principles of freedom and democracy.

Just as Jerrold condemned France in Algeria, so he condemns America in Mexico. He criticizes Polk's stand on extending territorial limits and deplores the destruction of cities and the thousands of lives lost in this imperialistic venture. He also attacks John Quincy Adams for "casting off his fair reputation as a statesman . . . and propounding the doctrines of a brigand" [37] when he favored going to war for Oregon. Because Adams said he stood upon the Bible in the Oregon dispute, Jerrold compares him to Sir Robert Harry Inglis who was delighted that the Governor-General of India gave religious justification for the slaughter of nine thousand Sikhs. One of the few Americans to receive praise from Jerrold in *Punch* was an obscure blacksmith named Elihu

Burritt who wrote a book entitled *Olive Leaves*, in which he made a proposal for peace between England and America. Jerrold praised the author for his honesty and common sense.

The most talked-about American in London in the year 1844 was a dwarf named Charles Stratton, better known as General Tom Thumb. When his manager, the notorious P. T. Barnum, arrived in Liverpool, he had premonitions of failure in this commercial adventure across the ocean. He determined that the only way to establish Tom Thumb financially was to make him the darling of fashion, trusting the common people to follow in the tracks of their betters; consequently, he directed all his efforts towards seeking the approval of Queen Victoria. Barnum's cunning led to Thumb's appearance at Buckingham Palace, where he so charmed the royal family that it received him three times. Victoria presented Thumb with several expensive souvenirs, among which was a gold pencil case with the initials "T.T." and his coat of arms engraved on it. His subsequent appearances at the Egyptian Hall brought thousands of people to watch the little man strut about in his famous imitation of Napoleon and to see his representation of Grecian statues. Even the Duke of Wellington, who frequently called at the Hall, was particularly amused by Thumb's Napoleonic pose. Sir Robert and Lady Peel, the dukes and duchesses of Buckingham, Bedford, and Devonshire, Daniel O'Connell, and Lord Chesterfield were special friends of Thumb.

But the historian's or biographer's account of Barnum's invasion of England little resembles that of Douglas Jerrold. His serial about Tom Thumb, entitled *The English in Little*,[38] appeared in *Punch* during the years 1846 and 1847 simultaneously alongside of Thackeray's *Snobs of England;* and though not as popular as Thackeray's series, it constituted the second most important attraction of the magazine for over half a year. The first paper explains that, because "the English have idolised a dwarf," the pigmy, "duly returning the compliment, paints 'The English in Little.'" Drawing upon current topics, Jerrold satirizes in this series the societies of both England and America. The dual satire is effectively achieved by having the series told in dialect from the first-person point of view of Tom Thumb. Jerrold specifically pokes fun at the gullibility of the English and at their preference for foreigners. Like the rash of imported French plays and foreign spectaculars, Tom Thumb overshadowed the English dramatists, including Jerrold. In earlier issues of *Punch* and in other journals, Jerrold vehemently crusaded against the pernicious effects of mere spectacle upon the legitimate drama.

By dangling Thumb like a rash puppet in the midst of Buckingham Palace and by making him raise the regal roof, Jerrold condemns royalty for lavishly favoring the foreign performer over many of England's gifted writers and artists. The aristocracy, upon whom Jerrold heaped the blame for most of England's ills, is also attacked in the series for neglecting the country's poor and for applauding the American visitor. Because of Jerrold's hatred for war and Toryism, Jerrold singles out the Duke of Wellington for especial ridicule. The characteristic frankness of Thumb is also used to expose the deplorable state of the drama, inhuman conditions found in the workhouses, and the general hypocrisy of English society.

Interwoven and contrasting with the preceding satire is a critical and satiric portrayal of American society. Specifically, Jerrold caricatures the vulgarity and egotistic patriotism of Americans, their pragmatic ethical standards, and the hypocrisy of a whole nation which proclaims itself to be a free republic but practices slavery. Nevertheless, one may discern beneath the satire Jerrold's respect for the forthrightness and stamina inherent in the American's brash independence.

In terms of Jerrold's announced prospectus, set forth in the first installment, to present Thumb's comments upon social institutions, virtues, vices, drama, literature, the English constitution, and government, Jerrold fails to develop the last three topics. To have fulfilled his broad promise, aimed at raising the expectations of his readers, would have required the series to be unduly long. Furthermore, because of the enormous success of Thackeray's *Snob Papers*, Jerrold suffered a loss of popularity for the first time in his career with *Punch*. These two factors, combined with pressures of writing for and editing other journals, contributed to the curtailment of the Thumb papers.

The first chapter by Thumb is devoted to revealing his egotistical character, and to his and Barnum's reaction on not receiving an invitation to the Palace. By a process of egotistical logic, Barnum tells Thumb that the queen has insulted the "Star-Spangled Banner" by not extending him an invitation. He reasons that Thumb is "the greatest, brightest star of that banner," and with that pun accuses the queen of an insult. Barnum's six-shooter patriotism is revealed when he plans to challenge Prince Albert to a gun duel in the name of the "Star-Spangled Banner." But English royalty is spared its blue blood when a note inviting Barnum and his protégé to Buckingham Palace arrives just in time. The two Americans are insulted again because the note says they must come to the palace by the back stairs. Jerrold contrives this situation in order to satirize America as a free republic through Thumb's comment: "At Washington there is no backstairs. When we want Mr. Polk, we don't stand knocking at the door; but just turn the handle and walk into the drawing-room; and if he's not there, into any other place in the house; and we should just like to catch him putting a bolt to any door on the premises" (Xl, 211). But the visitors suffer the indignity and take the back stairs, where they meet a "Lord-in-waitin," and Thumb, who asserts that he is writing for Americans, defines the gentleman as "a lord waiting for whatever he can get to better himself." The satire quickly reverts upon the Americans, however, as the queen offers Tom a cup of tea and asks if he wants brown or white sugar. This incident is clearly arranged for Jerrold's continued attack upon American slavery. Tom will take either sugar, "but if it isn't slave-grown, I'm a true republican, and won't touch a tarnation morsel" (Xl, 219).

In the next chapter, Jerrold depicts how much at ease the General is in Victoria's presence; for Jerrold caricatures him as the brash American who cannot respect royalty because he cannot understand it. Moreover, he expects the whole non-American world to cater to him only because he is an American: "I'll take the best they can give me, as if I was born for it, like an American citizen. I'm determined nothin shall surprise me. If Gracious Majesty gives me the crown of England to hold my marbles in, why, I'll keep a stiff upper lip; praps I'll say 'thankee,' praps I won't." (Xl, 235). As this chapter develops by Thumb's extending an invitation to the Queen to visit America, it becomes increasingly clear that Jerrold is greatly enjoying his confrontation of royalty with such brashness, inasmuch as he has allowed Thumb to progress from the back stairs to a friendly chat with Victoria about how she must eat the real Hominy Cake at Uncle Sam's fireside. With the gusto of a Nebraska farmer, Thumb tells her that in America all her "critters won't be cramped up," but may "grow and expand like corn cobs."

The satire gradually turns away from America as Thumb is used more as a device to satirize the English. For instance, when he first meets Prince Albert, he naïvely asks: "anything doin at the Playhouses?" At this question, Barnum's eyebrows rise like "the arches of Waterloo Bridge," and a Maid-of-Honor whispers in Thumb's ear: "not a word about them low places" (Xl, 239). Thumb is here simply a mouthpiece for Jerrold's satire of royalty for its failure to support the English drama by giving preference to respectable foreign operas and musicals. As a popular dramatist himself, Jerrold had a vested interest in the theater; he realized, as did Barnum, that royal approval often elicits popular demand. He also ridicules royalty's attitude toward the other arts by portraying a crowd of philosophers, artists, and musicians arriving at the palace by the back stairs, thus indirectly equating them with Barnum and Thumb. One of the imagined guests is Carlyle, who is described as the man who "teaches the Prince German and English from his own books, and both together."

The next chapter turns the satire back upon the Americans, as Thumb and Barnum take a catalogue of presents bestowed at the palace. In the course of their conversation, Thumb uses the term "game-cock" for "rooster." Barnum grows solemn and reminds Thumb that he is pure American and must always say "rooster": "I should never forgive myself if I'd brought you from the most enlightened nation of the airth to be contaminated by the vulgarity of Europe" (Xl, 257). After their presents are catalogued and ridiculed, Barnum discloses his motives for getting Thumb into the palace, and from this section it is evident that Jerrold saw through the cunning plans devised in Liverpool: "If Gracious Majesty gives a watch, in course the housemaid will give a thimble. It's example in high places that makes the true vally of monarchy."

After an absurd comparison of the Egyptian Hall with Exeter Hall that allows Jerrold to vent some of his notorious sarcasm upon the English clergy, he has Thumb digress upon Christmas in England for the New Year's number of *Punch*. It contains a mild satire of the annual cattle fair and the workhouses that make purchases there. Thumb explains "they are called Unions out of joke,

acause they break the weddin-ring in 'em, and part man and
wife" (Xll, 1). Here again, Thumb sounds much more like Mr.
Punch or Jerrold in his sarcastic word play.

The success of this essay, with its humorous and familiar references to English Christmases, dictated the following one, which
used the same device and had Thumb comment upon New Year's
Day and Twelfth-Cake art. But of wider significance is Barnum's
definition of modesty, which arose in response to the question,
"Why does John Bull like foreigners afore his own Britishers?"
Barnum's answer to this loaded question is that it all comes from
the Englishman's modesty. There follows Jerrold's analysis of the
essential difference in personality between the American and the
Englishman, an innate commercial vulgarity separating the two.
Barnum declares:

> . . . there is nothing—no moral pinte on the airth that money will
> not illustrate, if only you know how to set about it. Well, modesty is
> jist as stupid a thing as this; it is for all the world as if a full weight
> goolden sov'reign was to insist upon going for only nineteen shillins,
> and not a farden more. That is modesty; by which you will understand
> that modesty is always a thing that a man loses by. . . . Why it's as
> if a whole hog should beleetle himself down to a suckin pig. (Xll, 19)

Here is a savage caricature of the vulgar American who glibly
uses money even to illustrate moral problems. And, when one ap-
plies this pragmatic philosophy to Thumb, the implication is that
he is "a full weight goolden sov'reign" who is simply receiving his
just evaluation from the English. This application naturally makes
the philosophy that much more pernicious. Jerrold makes it clear
how he feels about Barnum not only by what he says but by his
vulgar style of phrasing delicate moral points: "Why it's as if a
whole hog should beleetle himself down to a suckin pig."

Having ridiculed Barnum's commercial mentality, Jerrold continues the theme in the next paper, which is devoted to illustrating
Thumb's vulgarity. The General says that, when the Mayor and
Aldermen come to dine with him, "jist to ryle 'em a bit, and to
show 'em the glory, and wealth, and independence of the freest
nation of all creation—let them cook *my* chop in a twenty-pound
Bank o' England note" (Xll, 39). As Barnum saw modesty in
terms of money, Thumb sees glory and independence in terms of
a twenty-pound note. But this portrait is more than simply a cari-

cature of a vulgar American because, as the essay goes on, it is
made plain that Thumb is very well aware of what he is doing. All
the time he is eating, he is relishing the fascinated stares of the
Mayor and Aldermen: "Well, I ses nothin; but with the end of my
knife, I takes the bank note off the chop, and throws it into the
silver dish." Thumb is portrayed as a commercial success and as a
money-seeking American whose self-awareness enables him to exploit his immodesty for financial gain. In short, Jerrold gives Barnum and Thumb credit for being the great showmen they are;
and he pictures them as one up on the wide-eyed English.

In the next paper, Jerrold presents Thumb's report of the great
public manifestation that greeted him as he departed for his performance at the Egyptian Hall. By presenting this picture of the
hullabaloo through the eyes of the feature attraction, Jerrold's satiric account scooped the ablest newsmen:

Well, the door was opened, and the Mayor and the Aldermen got
into their carriages and wheeled off, and the men in armour began to
trot, and the brass band to play "See, the Conquerin Hero comes!"—
it's always played to me and Wellington—and the people hooraed as
if they'd tear a hole in the sky above 'em. Then they began to screach
for Tom Thumb. "Where's the Gen'ral" they cried, "The Gen'ral—
the Gen'ral!" for they never seed me get in the chariot. "The Gen'ral!"
cried the men—and the women, the dear critters, I could hear their
voices like the ringin of so many dollars, cryin out, "Where's the
Darlin?" "the Duck?" "the Cherub?" "the Angel?" "the airthly Bird
of Paradise?" and I don't know what beside. For this is clear, I'd turned
all the critters' heads afore they'd seen me; and after they'd seen me
agin and agin, and kissed and kissed me, till my cheeks was wastin
away like a cake of Windsor soap, their heads had another twist, and
are goin on turnin and turnin at this present moment. How Barnum
did larf!—I felt the critter grinnin in his very pockets as he heard the
mob—and didn't I punch him with both my fists, and larf too! (Xll,
63)

This extremely vivid scene derives much of its effectiveness from
the satiric contrast between the wild jubilation and excitement of
the mob and the mercenary interpretation, equally jubilant,
placed upon that excitement by Thumb: "I could hear their voices
like the ringin of so many dollars. . . ." And his empathy with
Barnum is almost sinister: "I felt the critter grinnin in his very

pockets as he heard the mob. . . ." But, of course, all the crowd sees is his punching Barnum with both his fists, an innocent act of joyous affection. In one clamorous scene Jerrold has satirized the gullibility of the English people, the peculiar taste of its women, the heroic stature of the Duke of Wellington, and the greed of Barnum and Thumb. But the scene is not actually farfetched: Thumb's presence in public did cause uproarious crowds, and the women did enjoy kissing the little creature whenever they could get close enough.

The final installment of Thumb's account of the English simply relates how he recalled the days of Waterloo to Wellington and caused him to burst into tears. Then Thumb leaves England and writes to *Punch* that his next adventure will be to run for president of the United States.

It is hard to say why the *Snob Papers* surpassed *The English in Little* in popularity. As Anthony Trollope has pointed out, Thackeray's series is entirely too long, although this fault probably was not so apparent when the portraits appeared at weekly intervals. They try to be too comprehensive; and, says Trollope, Thackeray's "zeal was at last greater than his discrimination." [39] J. Y. T. Greig finds the series "too full of repetitions," its humor "often forced, and its wit flat." [40] One might add that Thackeray failed to unify the portraits. *The English in Little,* on the other hand, progresses from Barnum's arrival in London, through his rise to popular acceptance, to his departure for America. Unity is also obtained by having the serial told from the point of view of Tom Thumb.

In any event, the *Snob Papers* will always remain interesting for the light they shed on Thackeray's development from a journalist into a novelist. But comic journalism may profitably be considered an art in itself. A great body of humor lies unexplored in *Punch* magazine alone, not to mention numerous other journals. An examination of this material would certainly add to knowledge of the literary development of Victorian England, including a fuller understanding of eminent Victorians who grew up surrounded by a rich comic tradition. Furthermore, such a study may reveal a number of works capable of amusing readers today and of showing them that, while some Victorians were frozen between two worlds, one dead and the other powerless to be born, there were some who worked hard at the role of comic midwife.

IV   *Unmerry Old England*

One need only examine Friedrich Engels' book, *The Condition of the Working Classes in England in 1844*, based upon the government's own statistics and reports, to realize that Jerrold's England was not a merry one. A large percentage of his weekly essays were attacks upon the social injustices being mercilessly inflicted upon the poor and underprivileged. Although he welcomed industrial progress, represented by the steam engine, the sewing machine, and the factory system, he vigorously protested against its attendant abuses. While accepting the principle of capitalism, he spoke out against the unfair distribution of profits. Here he echoes his peers, Carlyle, Dickens and Ruskin, in their attacks upon the false god, Mammon, and the greed of the manufacturers. But Jerrold was an optimist who believed that, as time went on, the workingman would demand his share of the labor from "a few elder sons of luck and Mammon." [41]

Like his friend Thomas Hood, Jerrold deplored the sweatshops and looked forward to the passage of the Ten Hours Bill. He was appalled at the surrogate baby sitters like Godfrey's Cordial that were used to drug infants while their mothers worked all day in the mines. He campaigned loudly against Lord Brougham, when he favored the status quo and claimed the aristocracy had hardships comparable to the poor.

On the subject of the poor laws and the workhouse Jerrold, like Dickens in *Oliver Twist*, condemned the wicked abuses of the needy; and be culled numerous examples of cruelty in union workhouses from the newspapers in order to arouse public sympathy with the facts. A major theme of all his writings is the contrast between the rich and the poor. The very title of his novel, *St. Giles and St. James*, is indicative of his thinking along two lines that may never meet. He believed that the poor laws and workhouses were the dirty work of all political parties: "Tories, Whigs, and Radicals—for all ye, more or less, assisted at the work—gather round, and marvel at the automaton parent ye have fashioned." [42] He sees the poor-law atrocities being perpetuated by the callous legislators and complacent aristocracy.

A bold propagandist, he deliberately overstates and oversimplifies his position: the rich can do no good and the poor no evil. He humorously resolves this disparity of classes by heavy-handed satire: hang paupers from hooks and let them live on air, or push crowds of the poor over cliffs so that the poor may not always be with us. Over and over again, Jerrold reverts to the same theme of two conflicting classes, with the rich man always depicted as the villain. It is a theme similar to that expressed by Disraeli in *Sybil, or the Two Nations:* the rich and the poor are like two nations between whom there is no sympathy and who are as ignorant of each other's way of life as inhabitants of two distinct planets. Jerrold, however, blames only the rich for this lack of understanding and sympathy.

Jerrold carries this theme into all areas of society, and he claims that the law is clearly on the side of the aristocratic and the wealthy middle classes. The machinery of legal action was too costly and thus kept the poor man from his rightful protection; sometimes even innocent people, for lack of money, could not pay the fees necessary to indict the guilty. He vehemently protests and ridicules decisions rendered upon the poor in the courts as unfair and inhuman. He argues that the legal machine is oblivious to the human aspects of each case, and that the cruelty of the law courts is a sign of the times, commensurate with the callousness of legislators, factory bosses, and unscrupulous tradesmen. He singles out the London Alderman Sir Peter Laurie as a representative of gross stupidity and unfeeling inhumanity, and holds his judgments up to constant ridicule. Cases in which dishonest tradesmen, who were wealthy enough to pay their fines and go free, are contrasted with those in which innocent people were imprisoned for poverty.

Mark Lemon, the editor of *Punch,* set forth "The Moral of Punch" in its first number: "We are the advocates for the *correction* of offenders; but how many generous and kindly beings are there pining within the walls of a prison, whose only crimes are poverty and misfortune." [48] He expresses the hope that the time may soon arrive "when every prison shall be a palace of the mind —when we shall seek to instruct and cease to punish." Jerrold consistently supports this moral of *Punch.* He seeks out and exploits the inequality of justice in the professions, and portrays the lawyer as a self-seeking, unprincipled scoundrel who uses the law for self-aggrandizement. If there were ever an honest lawyer in England, one would not know it from Jerrold's writings. But such exaggeration and caricature are characteristics not only of his style but of the entire magazine, one particularly obvious in the cartoons. Leech's "Old Bailey Justice After Dinner" [44] is a devastating caricature of justice that shows seven fat magistrates in an after-dinner stupor brought on by gluttony and drink. The only vestige of justice visible is in the robes and wigs; and even here one of the men has his wig on backward so that the curls fall over his face.

Jerrold used the game laws and the severe penalties for breaking them to illustrate the aristocratic and legal oppression of the poor: the laws represent the rich man's greed and an aristocratic society's depraved values that place hares and pheasants before the welfare of the poor. As early as 1831, when he was writing for the *Athenaeum*, he called for the repeal of the game laws; and he continued writing against them years later in *Punch*, where other writers and artists joined in the attack.

Jerrold's views on society are actually very similar to those of Dickens. In 1843, Jerrold contributed an article to his new *Illuminated Magazine* called "Elizabeth and Victoria," in which he expressed his abhorrence of old institutions and held the past responsible for the present social abuses and iniquities. This same year Dickens wrote to Jerrold his enthusiastic approval of these views:

> It is very wise, and capital; written with the finest end of that iron pen of yours; witty, much needed, and full of truth. I vow to God that I think the parrots of society more intolerable and mischievous than its birds of prey. If ever I destroy myself, it will be in the bitterness of hearing those infernal and damnably good old times extolled. . . . I am writing a little history of England for my boy. . . . I have tried to impress upon him (writing, I daresay, at the same moment with you) the exact spirit of your paper. For I don't know what I should do if he were to get hold of any Conservative or High Church notions; and the best way of guarding against any such horrible result, is, I take it, to wring the parrots' necks in his very cradle. [45]

Dickens, who was equally enthusiastic about Jerrold's other writings, once remarked to him in a letter: "I have so steadily read you, and so selfishly gratified myself in always expressing the admiration with which your gallant truths inspired me, that I must not call it time lost." [46] And when Dickens read *The Chimes* in 1844, his first important pronouncement on the "Condition-of-England Question," Jerrold was among the select audience.

Even before Jerrold wrote for *Punch,* Jerrold was writing plays with social themes that interestingly parallel Dickens' early novels. In *The Mutiny of the Nore* (1830) the grievances of the mutineers are sympathetically developed; in *The Rent Day* (1832), he attacks absentee landlords who squander their oppressed tenants' money in London gambling parlors; in *The Golden Calf* (1832), he satirizes excessive deference to wealth and position; and in *The Factory Girl* (1832), he attacks the abuses of child labor in the weaving industry. Yet, like Dickens' early novels, these plays, while dramatizing and satirizing social abuses, do not attempt to offer serious commentary on oppressing social conditions. Jerrold's usual solution to the knots that he ties, as a critic of *The Factory Girl* pointed out, is simply "to have an extensive relationship discovered among the principal characters." [47] In other words, Jerrold "solves" the social problems, as he did the political ones, with literary devices that give insight into the interactions of the characters, instead of into the ostensible social abuse. The only other solution implied in his works is good will and fellowship among men, also a frequent theme in Dickens' novels.

In an essay Thackerary wrote for the *Times* on the sketches of John Leech, Thackeray best summarizes the central themes in Jerrold's social protest in *Punch:*

Mr. Leech surveys society from the gentleman's point of view. In old days, when Mr. Jerrold lived and wrote for that famous periodical, he took the other side; he looked up at the rich and great with a fierce, a sarcastic aspect, and a threatening posture, and his outcry, or challenge was: "Ye rich and great, look out! We, the people, are as good as you. Have a care, ye priests, wallowing on a tithe pig and rolling in carriages and four; ye landlords grinding the poor; ye vulgar fine ladies, bullying innocent governesses, and what not—we will expose your vulgarity; we will put down your oppression; we will vindicate the nobility of our common nature," and so forth. A great deal was to be said on the Jerrold side, a great deal was said—perhaps, even a great deal too much.[48]

Jerrold's attacks upon the London Alderman, Sir Peter Laurie, and on capital punishment are typical of his vigorous crusade in behalf of the poor and oppressed. In 1841 the *Times* recorded in a few small paragraphs the case of William Simmons, an unemployed tailor, who was charged by a policeman with having attempted to cut his own throat with a razor. When Alderman Laurie asked Simmons why he tried to commit suicide, he replied that he was in a perishing condition and could get nothing to do. Then Laurie said: "Suicides and attempts, or apparent attempts, to commit suicide very much increase, I regret to say. I know that a morbid humanity exists, and does much mischief, as regards the practice. I shall not encourage attempts of the kind, but shall punish them; and I sentence you to the treadmill for a month, as a rogue and vagabond. I shall look very narrowly at the cases of persons brought before me on such charges." [49]

Jerrold used this case as the basis for one of his early "Q" papers,[50] in which he attempts to fasten down in the person of Alderman Laurie the evil attendant upon egotism and callousness that is diffused throughout society. The rest of the essay is devoted to a consideration of the relative values of life, as viewed first by the rich and powerful, and then by the poor and weak. Here is Jerrold's old theme of the rich versus the poor explored through an analysis of their radically different attitudes towards existence. To the man of independent wealth and sound body, life is "a realm of fairies, with attending sprites to perform his every compassable wish." To an alderman, it is "a fine, dignified, full-bellied, purple-faced creature, in a furred and violet-coloured gown." But to the Paisley weaver and to the famine-stricken crowds of Bolton, life is worse than death; it is that daily tyrant "with that withered face, sunken eye, and shrivelled lip."

Jerrold seems to suggest that Laurie's sentence upon tailor Simmons was unjust because it failed to take into account the relative values of human life and was therefore lacking in sympathy and compassion. Simmons was innocent in Jerrold's eyes because he attempted to commit suicide for reasons justified by his desperate view of life; his actions can be considered criminal only from the unsympathetic point of view of the comfortably rich. The essay concludes that "there is a better remedy for such desperation than the treadmill. The surest way for the rich and powerful of the world to make the poor man more careful of his life is to render it of greater value to him." Despite the sarcasm and exaggeration, there is a serious attempt, however crude and biased, to go below the surface of court sentences in an effort to understand "the social insensibility of the day."

Jerrold repeats this theme in another "Q" paper two years later, when Laurie is caricatured as "The Pig-Skin Solomon." [51] The essay was touched off by Laurie's statement that he never knew a convicted thief to become a reformed man. Jerrold portrays Laurie as a monkey to represent his complete inability to understand the people he condemns. Seven years after his first article on Laurie, Jerrold still ridicules him for his past statements. Not only is the same theme of his callous, imperceptive, and absurd judgments repeated, but once again he is an inmate of the zoo in an essay cast in the form of a letter written to the London alderman by the Zebra of Surrey Zoological Gardens, the rationale being that the zebra is essentially "a Jackass in a fine coat." From there, it is reasoned: "How many folks there are whose brayings would never be listened to if not uttered in the finery of office and fine trappings." [52]

The statement that Laurie made over five years ago about the impossibility of a convicted thief ever becoming a reformed man is resurrected. By a series of allusions to people and professions dedicated to reforming the criminal, Jerrold sarcastically sides with Laurie. John Howard, the prison reformer, is pitied for his "foolish belief in the divine nature of man"; Elizabeth Fry, instead of visiting jails, would have been better employed "superintending her pickles and her jams at home"; and the "absurd expense" of prison parsons and schoolmasters must be abolished. The zebra, to whom these opinions are attributed, concludes by advising Laurie to rid society of philanthropy: "for the less that's paid to try to reform thieves the more shillings people will be able to afford to come and see—Your obedient Servant and Admirer, the Zebra."

Four years after Jerrold began writing his satires on Alderman Laurie, Dickens published *The Chimes*, in which Laurie was caricatured as Alderman Cute. The satire, which is remarkably similar to Jerrold's, focuses upon Cute's ruling passion to "Put Down!" Among the things, he would "put down" are distressed wives, boys without shoes, wandering mothers, sick children, and babies. He lectures to Meg: " 'And if you attempt, desperately, and ungratefully, and impiously, and fraudulently attempt, to drown yourself, I'll have no pity for you, for I have made up my mind to Put all sucide Down! If there is one thing,' said the Alderman, with his self-satisfied smile, 'on which I can be said to have made

up my mind more than on another, it is to Put suicide down.' " [53]
Alderman Laurie's notoriety, however, was first achieved
through the dedicated efforts of *Punch* and of Jerrold in particular, to whom Dickens is probably indebted for his caricature.

In 1832, housebreaking, horse stealing, sheep stealing, and the
coining of false money ceased to be capital offenses. After 1838
and for the rest of the century, no person was hanged except for
murder or (until 1861) attempted murder. On the other hand,
transportation as a substitute for capital punishment was near its
end in 1841 because English supporters of systematic colonization
did not want the colonies full of convicts. Therefore, most radical
reformers focused their attacks upon capital punishment.

After witnessing the public execution of François Courvoisier at
Newgate, Thackerary wrote his influential article "Going to See a
Man Hanged," which appeared in *Fraser's Magazine* (1840). He
re-creates with appalling vividness the picture of the sadistic
crowds who attended the execution to be amused and then gives
his personal reactions of horror and disgust at the actual hanging:
"It seems to me that I have been abetting an act of frightful wickedness and violence, performed by a set of men against one of
their fellows; and I pray to God that it may soon be out of the
power of any man in England to witness such a hideous and de-
grading sight." [54] The article concludes with Thackeray's rebuttal
of the usual arguments put forth to justify capital punishment. In
his *Punch* essay, Jerrold uses not only the same logic but the same
technique of first presenting a vivid picture of horror that emo-
tionally disposes the reader to accept more readily the logical conclusions.

Dickens was also violently opposed to capital punishment; and,
after witnessing the execution of Mr. and Mrs. Manning, he wrote
two letters to the *Times* protesting against public hangings. He
argued that such exhibitions had only a hardening and debasing
influence on the spectators and that, from the moment a murderer
was convicted, he should be kept from the curious visitors and
from the reporters who then reported his sayings and doings in
the Sunday papers. He suggested, as an alternative, that the convicted murderers be executed privately within prison walls. As
will be shown shortly, Dickens' protest is almost identical with
Jerrold's point of view in *Punch*. Nevertheless, Jerrold resented
Dickens' compromising in the slightest degree on the *principle* of

abolishing capital punishment and broke off his friendship with
him. For a number of months they did not see each other, until
finally Jerrold took the initiative in making up.

Mark Lemon outlined *Punch's* position on the subject of capital
punishment:

> We now come to the last great lesson of our motley teacher—the
> gallows! that accursed tree which has its *root* in injuries. How clearly
> *Punch* exposes the fallacy of that dreadful law which authorises the
> destruction of life! *Punch* sometimes destroys the hangman: and why
> not? Where is the divine injunction against the shedder of man's blood
> to rest? None *can* answer! To us there is but *one* disposer of life. At
> other times *Punch* hangs the devil: this is as it should be. Destroy the
> principle of evil by increasing the means of cultivating the good, and
> the gallows will then become as much a wonder as it is now a jest.[55]

Jerrold extends Lemon's "great lesson" in his attacks against
those who argue that the gallows set a moral example, the clergymen who support capital punishment, and the press that exploits
the lives of murderers for the popular taste. Outside of the attack
on the clergy and the unequivocal demand for the total abolition
of capital punishment, Dickens' views are identical with Jerrold's.
A brief look at Jerrold's first line of attack shows his rhetorical
approach to his subject.

In countering the argument that capital punishment serves a
moral example to discourage potential murders, Jerrold takes the
specific execution of a much-publicized murderer named Tawell
in order to analyze the "moral lesson." Since most people must
first learn of the execution before a moral lesson can be set, he
turns to the newspaper accounts of Tawell's life in prison up to
the time of his execution: "We are called into the cell of the assas-
sin; we are required to give earnest attention to his every look—
his every syllable—to note down the cut and colour of his clothes;
to chronicle in our memory what he eats and what he drinks,—
that we may, with all our heart and all our soul, the more intensely loathe and abominate the 'deep damnation" of his guilt.
The more we know of the pettiest doings of a murderer, the
greater our horror of murder! Our virtue is marvelously strengthened by the gossip of the condemned cell." [56] He denounces the
Court Circular, the *Pictorial Times,* and the *Standard* for giving
the grotesque details of a murderer's life; and Jerrold wittily sums

up the utilitarian character of such reporting: "we turn a murderer into a commodity, and open an account with homicide." [57]

Even the cartoons in *Punch* satirized the press; one appears within the text of Jerrold's first paper on Tawell and is probably aimed at the *Pictorial Times*. It shows a ragged boy standing at a newsstand:

Newsvender: Now, my man, what is it?
Boy: I vonts a nillustrated newspaper with a norrid murder and a likeness in it.

A reproduction of the murderer's portrait is printed, Jerrold argues, "that a likeness of the abhorred miscreant may find its way into all families for the especial Sabbath delight and edification of ladies and children." [58] Here Jerrold expresses the strong Victorian ethic that women and children are to be protected from coarse and ugly facts, a point of view which helped to distinguish *Punch* from the vulgar comic journals that preceded it. When the Sunday papers feature macabre details of murder it becomes difficult to supervise family reading; and *Punch* strove always, as has been observed, to supply the family with a selected subject matter that would be wholly acceptable within the Victorian household.

If there was any one oppressed group on whose behalf Jerrold fought vigorously it was the governesses of England, or, as he called them, the "Sisters of Misery." He began his defense in "Punch's Complete Letter Writer" and renewed it with greater force in 1848, the same year that Charlotte Brontë's *Jane Eyre* depicted a governess as a woman of intelligence, sensibility, and deep feeling. During the first half of the century, the subject of the governess's social standing, duties, privileges, and salary was frequently disputed in the newspapers and magazines. Unmarried girls in middle-class families who were forced to work, or girls of upper-class families that were suddenly impoverished, turned to the only respectable way open to them to earn a living and became governesses. The majority of applicants lacked the qualifications of Jane Eyre but were desperate to salvage their self-respect. Aware of this situation, as well as the degradation that fell to any woman who endeavored to support herself, those who hired governesses paid unjustly low wages and increased the duties and working hours. Governesses were often treated with scornful patronage or veiled contempt because they committed the unforgivable sin of falling from social grace.

Punch initiated slashing attacks upon the numerous advertisements for governesses in the magazines and newspapers. Jerrold devoted four letters in "Punch's Complete Letter Writer" to the subject, in which he satirizes the unreasonable demands placed by ladies upon governesses and the unjust compensation awarded them. Honoria Asphalt writes to her friend Dorothea Flint that she is in need of a governess but laments that some clever gentleman has not invented a teaching machine to replace governesses, "a class of individuals who have no standing in society, and are nevertheless continually at one's elbow." Honoria is made to satirize the prevalent genteel attitude when she regrets "there is no teaching a governess that she is nothing more than a servant; a person hired for wages to polish the minds of your children, just in the same manner as Molly polishes your rosewood and mahogany. . . ." Honoria has already brought about the ruin of her last governess for her "baseness" in reading Dickens' *A Christmas Carol* in her home, a book Honoria knew "to be aimed at the best interests of good society."

Mrs. Flint's idea of a good governess is that she be a "sort of machine ordained by Providence to await the behests of those ordained above her." She cannot see why, on an annual salary of twenty pounds, out of which she has only to buy clothes, a governess cannot save a sufficiency for her declining age. Mrs. Flint explains that she deducts any day's or week's wages for which a governess is ill in order to outwit her artifice.

Finally there is a letter from a young lady desirous of an engagement as family governess. Her father's fortune having suddenly been reversed, she must now earn a living. She explains her noble concept of her new responsibilities and concludes: "As her mission is a noble one, respect and courtesy are hers by right." [59] Her patient, quiet labors will lead to good daughters, good wives, and good mothers. In such fashion does Jerrold use Mary Wilton's letter to phrase his reasonable argument on behalf of all the Sisters of Misery. The entire letter is unusual for its restraint, its humility, and its calm, incisive argument. Jerrold could spend his wrath in caustic and blunt satire in the first three letters written by the "villains," and contrast them with the congenial nobility and sweet reasonableness of Mary Wilton.

In 1845, Jerrold renewed his attack but changed his tactics. He continued to write in the guise of a governess, but this time he did so in answer to actual advertisements printed in the newspapers. His article entitled "Sisters of Misery" is typical. He quotes an advertisement from the *Times:* "Wanted, in a *Gentleman's* family, a *Lady*, who can be well recommended as Nursery Governess. She must be fond of children, clever with her needle, active, intelligent, and good-tempered in the discharge of her duties. *No salary will be given.* Travelling expenses and washing paid, with every domestic comfort." The advertisement is carefully worded to secure a "lady," and the fact that no salary is offered works both to reinforce the dignity of the position and to save the gentleman's money. Jerrold's sarcastic reply, which he offers as a form letter for all governesses, charges that they are being financially abused on the pretext of social respectability: "You state, Sir, and I admire the frankness—that 'no salary will be given.' I can fully understand, Sir, that the delightful privilege of dwelling under your roof, and enjoying the pure moral atmosphere of your hearth, must exceed any value to be awarded by the coined dross of this selfish world. How happy am I that, possessing a sufficient competence of my own, I may give myself up heart, and soul, and pocket, to the formation of the minds of your children, and to the daily execution of your needlework." [60]

An indication as to how low the condition of the governesses had fallen is the establishment in the early 1840's of the Governesses' Benevolent Institution. The energetic leader of ths organization, the Reverend David Laing, soon realized what Jerrold, in his humanitarian exuberance, failed to see—that these women could not command adequate salaries unless properly educated for their work and that most of them were not. Laing cooperated with Amelia Murray, who was collecting funds for Queen's College; and, when the school was established, they provided a committee to supervise and examine ladies of rank and talent who wanted to become governesses. Jerrold's efforts were aimed at stirring public opinion, not at offering practical solutions; but, if it had not been for conscientious men like him who crusaded for the right of women to support themselves and demand decent wages, the larger issue of women's rights might have been realized more slowly. As President of the Whittington Club, Jerrold not only allowed women to become members but demanded their right to vote on the executive council. In this controlled, progressive little world, at least, he set up a model of reform which anticipated the social changes to come about years later in Victorian society at large.

The poor are always the underdog crushed by wealth, class, tradition, and religious hypocrisy. Since satire is essentially destructive and need not offer alternatives or solutions, it is not surprising to discover that Jerrold has no specific political or social gospel to put forward. He does, however, express his humanitarian idealism by envisioning a reconciliation of the rich and the poor. The essay is notable because it contrasts directly with the hundreds of sarcastic and satiric essays he wrote on the same theme. Jerrold speaks as the character most like himself, Mr. Punch:

Surely there will come a time when the Rich and the Poor will fairly meet, and have a great human talk upon the matter; will hold a parliament of the heart, and pass acts that no after selfishness and wrong— on either side—shall repeal! The rich will come—not with cricket-balls or quoits in their hands—to make brotherhood with the Poor; but touched with the deep conviction that in this world the lowest created man has a solemn part to play, directed to solemn ends; that he is to be considered and cared for, in his condition, with tenderness, with fraternal benevolence; that there is something more than alms due from the high to the low; that human sympathy can speak otherwise than by the voice of money; and that, too, in at once a loftier and sweeter tone of hope and comforting.[61]

Jerrold's usual bitter and satiric tone has changed into serious ethical moralizing, which gives the essay the character of a sermon. "A parliament of the heart" clearly indicates that Jerrold, like Dickens, believed in sentiment and good will as the solution to the social evils of the day. As Jerrold had said earlier, the great social vice of his age was the lack of sympathy for one's fellow man. The idealistic prediction of a reconciliation also owes something to Carlyle, who constantly preached that the "cash nexus" was not enough to cement true human relationships and that there must be instead a brotherhood based upon fraternal benevolence. The sentiment is paraphrased by Jerrold when he writes that "human sympathy can speak otherwise than by the voice of money."

V   *A Victorian Curtain Lecturer*

The most popular and successful of all Jerrold's writings was *Mrs. Caudle's Curtain Lectures,* serialized in *Punch* between January and November, 1845. The popularity of the *Lectures* increased the magazine's circulation by leaps and bounds. Week by week newsagents would ascertain whether or not there was another installment included before deciding upon how many copies they would require. Margaret Caudle and her hen-pecked husband, Job, became familiar names in almost every household; and the Caudles soon began to appear on commercial advertisements for items as various as soap and liver pills. They even turned up on stoneware gin bottles. One such bottle shows Mrs. Caudle in her nightcap and bears her familiar prelude to Job's insomnia: "No, Mr. Caudle, I shall not go to sleep." Even Jerrold's coworkers on *Punch* capitalized upon the popularity of his serial, as evidenced by John Leech's cartoon depicting Lord Brougham as Mrs. Caudle and Lord Chancellor Lyndhurst as Job. Unscrupulous publishers began using pirated versions of the *Lectures,* and hack playwrights were busily adapting them into comic sketches and musicals that were played to laughing thousands both in London and in the provinces.

A writer for the *New Monthly Magazine* best summarizes the contemporary reaction to Jerrold's unexpected success:

. . . there was truth to nature in the matter and manner of Job Caudle's narrative. On the mere closeness to truth of his "plain statement" was founded its success as a hit, a very palpable hit. Henpecked husbands could not see that it was a bit overdone; others, more happily mated, more equally matched, could see on the face of it, in defect of any personal experience on their own part, a self-asserting, self-evident verisimilitude; and bachelors of every age and degree had an intuitive conviction that the thing was nature itself, and that had a short-hand writer been behind the curtain he could not have reproduced the curtain lecture with a more literal fidelity.[62]

Thackeray, in an anonymous review of the *Curtain Lectures* for the *Morning Chronicle,* reserved his highest praise for the verisimilitude of the Caudles: "The couple have become real living personages in history, like Queen Elizabeth, or Sancho Panza, or Parson Adams, or any other past character, who, false or real once, is only imaginary now, and for whose existence we have only the word of a book. And surely to create these realities is the greatest triumph of a fictitious writer—a serious or humorous poet." [63]

Many women did not accept Mrs. Caudle as an entertaining portrayal of their sex but grew furious at her creator and let him know their extreme displeasure in indignant letters and public rebuttals. Mrs. Anne Marsh-Caldwell, one of the most popular minor novelists of the 1840's and 1850's, attacks Jerrold in an early chapter of *Emilia Wyndham* for setting an example of incivility for men to follow: "Any vulgar penny-a-liner can draw Mrs. Caudle, and publish her in a popular journal; and with such success that she shall become a by-word in families, and serve as an additional reason for that rudeness and incivility, that negligent contempt, with which too many Englishmen still think it their prerogative, as men and true-born Britons, to treat their wives." [64] The heroine of *Emilia Wyndham* undergoes a number of torments inflicted upon her by a selfish and unworthy father, who made the life of his daughter, and still more that of his wife, unbearably miserable. Mrs. Marsh obviously intended to counter the one-sided view of marriage in the *Curtain Lectures* by presenting a detestable husband. At the conclusion of the novel she addresses the reader: "is it not just possible, think you, that *some* of the discomforts of married life—a *very* small proportion, of course—might be ameliorated, if husbands now and then received a lesson in their turn, and learned to correct themselves as well as wives?" [65]

In 1846 *Punch* "reviewed" the *Curtain Lectures* by pretending to quote a passage from *Emilia Wyndham:*

"What!" said Emilia, her peach-down cheek glowing with emotion; "You do not like *Mrs. Caudle?* Well, I never! Woman as I am, I adore it. All the springs—the springes I should rather say—of woman's nature are so deliciously, so delicately developed in that love of a book. 'Twould have beguiled Eve herself in her banishment. She would have looked into its limpid page, and, as erst at the fountain, when but a day old—alas! how soon we women take to mirrors!—she would have seen the reflection of her very soul. Well, if ever I marry—and here Emilia looked with ecstatic wickedness in the eyes of her lover—if ever I marry, I should wish no better bridal present than *Mrs. Caudle,* bound in Hymeneal satin!"

Henry—what could he do?—instantaneously whipped his arm round
Emilia's waist, and looking into her blue orbs, exclaimed, in a voice
tremulous with passion, "Emilia, thou shalt have it." [66]

In the preface to the 1852 edition of the *Curtain Lectures,* Jerrold says that many women, in wonder, pity, and reproof, have
asked him, "What could have made you think of Mrs. Caudle?
How could such a thing have entered any man's mind?" His answer is that she simply popped into his head as he was dreamily
watching a group of schoolboys in a playground: "One moment
there was no living object save those racing, shouting boys; and
the next, as though a white dove had alighted on the pen-hand of
the writer, there was—Mrs. Caudle." [67] One simply cannot help
speculating, however, that she might also have arisen from the
author's own household. When Mrs. Caudle attempts to wheedle
from Job his secret oath as a Mason, for example, one recalls that
Jerrold himself was Mason and assuredly must have suffered a
similar inquisition.

In the *Punch Almanac* for 1845 there appeared on the January
page the adaptation of a popular advertisement: "Worthy of attention./Advice to persons about to marry,—Don't." This notice
aptly preceded the first installment of the *Curtain Lectures* and
prophetically suggested its moral. As the title of the serial indicates, all the lectures are given in bed; the story progresses
through Mrs. Caudle's complaints and through shifting the location of the bedroom. Job is lectured each night because Margaret
knew that he "was too much distracted by his business as toyman
and doll merchant to digest her lessons in the broad day."

The first twenty-three lectures are given at home, in London.
During the course of these nightly harangues, one is introduced to
two other characters who figure largely in the serial, Harry Prettyman and his sister Sarah. Harry is Job's devil-may-care friend,
who causes him to stay out too late drinking and smoking. Miss
Prettyman is bowed to by Job on the streets, attends the Caudles'
wedding anniversary (which Mrs. Caudle interprets as a morbid
desire on her part to see how she would someday like the house
and the children), and becomes Job's partner at whist.

The next four lectures are given as the Caudles travel on their
vacation from Herne Bay to Margate to France and back home.
Two more lectures follow when Mrs. Caudle again grows restless

and desires a respectable country cottage, which, of course, she obtains; and the last seven scoldings are given in the pastoral setting of the "Turtle-Dovery." After becoming chilled while wearing her thin shoes, Mrs. Caudle grows deathly ill and dies—but not before lecturing Job on the impropriety of Miss Prettyman's visit, and stating in her final moment of self-pity that she "sha'n't be in her way long."

Although consisting basically of loosely connected psychological episodes, the serial has unity. Mrs. Caudle's suspicion of Job's fidelity, aroused by Miss Prettyman, who continually looms in the background as a marital threat, adds an element of suspense. And Margaret's self-pity, announced early in the serial by such typical statements as, "I know that I'm sinking every day" and "when I'm gone, we shall see how your second wife will look after your buttons," prepares the reader for the only psychologically satisfying conclusion—her actual death. The action is confined almost exclusively within the minds of the characters, and the effect of movement obtained by the several changes of scene is restricted by the exclusive focus upon the bedroom as the center of the Caudles' world.

Using a framed narrative, Jerrold reports that Job recorded only the best thirty-six lectures out of his thirty years of marriage, which presumably means that 10,914 lectures were judiciously rejected. When Job died, he left his manuscript along with enough money for its future publication; and Jerrold, acting as the anonymous editor, expresses the hope that he has "done justice to both documents," that is, to the lectures and Job's comments upon them. Thus one finds an Introduction, written by the anonymous editor; the lectures, as spoken by Mrs. Caudle; a short comment by Job appended to each lecture; and a postscript in which the anonymous editor humorously defends womankind at the conclusion of the lectures.

The role of the editor allows Jerrold to describe objectively Job's character so as to prepare the reader for Mrs. Caudle's wild distortions of it. More obviously, it allows him to explain who wrote the lectures and why, as well as to provide other necessary background information. Finally, the role enables him to affect sympathy with womankind by stating at the end that he never can believe the slander that all women have in their veins "one drop . . . of Caudle."

Job's authorial comments are usually of a mechanical nature, relating how either she or he finally fell asleep. Sometimes, however, the tailpiece is psychologically related to the lecture and presents an amusing consequence of it. After a long scolding for having lent an acquaintance the family umbrella, Job tells that he at length fell asleep and dreamt that "the sky was turned into green calico, with whalebone ribs; that, in fact, the whole world turned round under a tremendous umbrella."

Each lecture is cast in a form that closely parallels the dramatic monologue, and one gets Job's reactions only through his wife. His comments are usually indicated by italics in Mrs. Caudle's endless flow of words. When she accuses him of drinking and singing in a tavern, for instance, one learns of his weak remonstrance by Mrs. Caudle's repetition of his defense: *"You never sing?"* Taken a lecture at a time, the form seems entirely natural; for Job's comments serve as fuel for her fiery monologue.

Most of the lectures are written according to a basic formula: the theme of each lecture is stated at the outset; Mrs. Caudle then begins her harangue, which invariably includes how some innocent act of Job has caused her and the children to suffer; and Job makes two or three mild remonstrances that agitate her still further until finally she or Job falls asleep. A number of variations on the pattern, however, keep it from becoming tedious. When Margaret wants her mother to come to live with them, she reverses her usual approach; instead of nagging Job to sleep, she takes a positive view and declares how her mother will prepare his favorite dishes and save them money by brewing beer at home. Sometimes the variation comes by a surprise ending to a lecture. Usually Mrs. Caudle's theme, no matter how much it exaggerates Job's innocent actions, is based on fact: he does stay out late, he does lend the family umbrella. One night, however, he is severely lectured for putting up bail for his friend Harry Prettyman. Job finally manages to get a word in to explain that it was not Harry but her own brother for whom he put up bail, and Mrs. Caudle goes to sleep amidst repentant tears.

The *Curtain Lectures* satisfy a desire for realistic portrayal of character in humor, which Carlyle formulated in his essay on Jean Paul Richter in 1827 and which is repeated by Thackeray, G. H. Lewes, and later critics during the century. They also satisfy the Victorians' insistence upon sympathy in humor. Not only is Mrs.

Caudle a convincing character, but the entire family life of the
Caudles emerges, in Thackeray's words, "the most queer, minute,
and amusing picture of English middle-class life." Thackeray attests further to the realism of the portrayal:

> Almost all the events and perplexities of Cockney domestic economy
> pass before her . . . a foreigner, or a student in the twentieth century,
> may get out of her lectures as accurate pictures of London life as we
> can get out of the pictures of Hogarth. Caudle's friends, and habits,
> and predilections; his cozy evenings with the Skylarks—his attachment
> to punch—his struggles for a latch key—his natural and manly hatred
> for cold mutton—the manner in which the odious habit of smoking
> grows upon him and masters him, are here exposed with the most
> frightful distinctness. There must be thousands of Caudles in this town
> who drank punch and annoyed their wives with tobacco-smoke last
> night.[68]

The verisimilitude of the serial is rendered both by the selection
of subject matter and by Mrs. Caudle's manner of speech. All the
characters—Job, his wife, and his friends—are drawn from the
middle or working class of the 1840's. They are all without excep-
tional endowments and have lived through the ordinary experiences of love, marriage, and parenthood. Life is rather unhappy
and dull for them, and their world is largely limited to domestic
affairs. The subject matter of Mrs. Caudle's lectures more precisely discloses the limits of their world that comprises financial
squabbles, mother-in-law problems, Job's smoking, finding a prosperous godfather for "Number Six," and obtaining a cottage in the
suburbs as a means of acquiring respectability. The most extraordinary event in the life of the Caudles is their trip to France; and,
after being there only a day, Mrs. Caudle, who always longed to
visit Paris, declares—"You know, Caudle, I'm never happy when
I'm away from home. . . . No, home's my comfort; I never want
to stir over the threshold, and you know it." [69]

The "low" subject matter of the *Curtain Lectures* contrasts with
the high society of the "silver-fork novels," and the confined bedroom setting contrasts with the adventure stories of Frederick
Marryat. The very choice of a bedroom for the setting and the
intimacy of marriage for the theme provided a release from prudery, but it was also open to the charge of indelicacy. The prevail-

ing prudish attitude is clearly set forth in Mrs. Sarah Ellis' preface
to her volume *The Wives of England:*

> The greatest difficulty of my task, however, has been to me the lay-
> ing bare, as it were, before the public eye, the privacy of married life—
> of that life whose sorrows the heart alone can know, and with whose
> joys it is the universal privilege of all who share them, that no stranger
> shall intermeddle. This difficulty, of the extent of which I was not fully
> aware before commencing the work, has sometimes thrown a hesitancy
> —I had almost said a delicacy—in the way of writing with the strength
> which the occasion demanded; and I could not but feel that the sub-
> ject itself was one better calculated for confidential fireside intercourse,
> than for a printed volume.[70]

Mrs. Caudle's rhetoric attests to her unique personality. Her
speech consists of plain statements in simple sentences, expressive
of a wide range of moods, strategically deployed against her de-
fenseless husband. One has, for example, the following variations
of tone as she attempts to wheedle from Job his secret oath as a
Mason:

> Caudle, you shan't close your eyes for a week—no, you shan't—
> unless you tell me some of it. Come, there's a good creature; there's a
> love. I'm sure, Caudle, I wouldn't refuse you anything—and you know
> it, or ought to know it by this time. I only wish I had a secret! To
> whom should I think of confiding it, but to my dear husband? I should
> be miserable to keep it to myself and you know it. Now, Caudle?
> Was there ever such a man? A man, indeed! A brute!—yes, Mr.
> Caudle, an unfeeling, brutal creature, when you might oblige me, and
> you won't. (18)

She threatens, flatters, cajoles, and condemns, but to no avail. The
dramatic potential of such a character, who gradually convinces
the reader that people talked, acted, and thought like her, is obvious.

Jerrold's ambiguous attitude toward the Caudles also contributes to their credibility. In his writings on social and political
themes, he consistently sided with the economically oppressed
lower class. Now he sympathizes with the psychologically oppressed Job, who is presented as an object of both pity and con-

tempt. Jerrold does not identify completely with the husband, and he obviously at times relished exercising his own powers of invective through Mrs. Caudle. The ambiguity adds another dimension of reality to their characters to the degree that it parallels the mixed feelings one experiences toward actual people.

Although Job expresses sympathy toward his wife only after she dies, calling her his "sainted creature," Jerrold carefully enlarges her character with pathos. When she tries to persuade Job to spend the vacation at Margate, she declares, "the ocean always seems to me to open the mind. I see nothing to laugh at; but you always laugh when I say anything. Sometimes at the seaside— specially when the tide's down—I feel so happy: quite as if I could cry" (60). This pathos comes as a shock to the reader, who has long been accustomed to think of Mrs. Caudle as an unfeeling shrew. Suddenly to be made aware that she possesses a sensibility revitalizes her as a character, and the subsequent lectures are all colored by this new understanding. Mrs. Caudle's final lecture, delivered from her deathbed, eschews sentimentality in favor of genuine pathos: "And after all, we've been very happy. It hasn't been my fault, if we've ever had a word or two, for you couldn't help now and then being aggravating; nobody can help their tempers always,—especially men. Still we've been very happy, haven't we, Caudle?" (96).

The typical Victorian family and the social virtue of respectability are the two elements of middle-class life that the *Curtain Lectures* most thoroughly satirize. Because values have undergone a tremendous change since the 1840's, it is helpful to reconstruct the picture of the typical Victorian household as gathered from conduct manuals, newspapers, and fiction of the era. The basic pattern for middle-class families was the young queen and her steadily filling nursery, her earnest husband, and their domestic felicity. The father was the unquestioned master of the home, in the sense that he alone had any legal standing: his wife and children ranked among his legal possessions. The woman was the center of the home, and she built her life around her family. The solid, stable Victorian home has by now become legendary and its ritual is well known: the gathering of the whole household for family prayers, the attendance together at church on Sunday morning, the reading aloud in the evening, and the annual family vacation, usually a seaside holiday.

The home was felt to be both a peaceful refuge from the anxieties of modern life and a shelter for those moral and spiritual values which the spirit of commerce was threatening to destroy. Ruskin equated the home with a sacred temple: "This is the true nature of home—it is the place of Peace; the shelter, not only from injury, but from all terror, doubt, and division." [71] In the recoil from the city, the home assumed qualities of the pastoral and became a country of peace and innocence where life was kind and duty natural. Indeed, Mrs. Sarah Ellis, who wrote a series of standard manuals during the late 1830's and early 1840's (*Daughters of England, Wives of England,* and *Women of England*), contended in them that, since the life of business tends to debase the mind by making its goals materialistic, a wife should be solicitous to advance her husband's intellectual, spiritual, and moral nature. She should be "a companion who will raise the tone of his mind from . . . low anxieties, and vulgar cares" and will "lead his thoughts to expatiate or repose on those subjects which convey a feeling of identity with a higher state of existence beyond this present life." [72] Ruskin writes that a wife must be "enduringly, incorruptibly good; instinctively, infallibly wise . . . with the passionate gentleness of an infinitely variable, because infinitely applicable, modesty of service." [73]

Domestic felicity was also portrayed in fiction, where the home gradually became sentimentalized and the wife was given wings with which to fly above the debased world of pots and pans. The very title of Coventry Patmore's long poem *The Angel in the House* suggests that married love was more than mortal. Dickens, too, presents an idealized and sentimentalized picture of marriage in David Copperfield and Agnes Wickfield. A number of other Victorian authors showed that the love between a man and a woman frequently transcended mortality and that, when one partner died, romantic love continued in heaven. When Mrs. Caudle dies, Job calls her "that angel now in heaven," but that angel, instead of fostering eternal romantic love, continues to harass Job with her lectures from the grave.

Jerrold's *Curtain Lectures* helped bring fiction to terms with real life, for he not only satirized the ideal Victorian home but too clearly portrayed families who fell short of the ideal. Thackeray suggested that the lectures be read and collected in a volume because "they form a body of conjugal morality." Like thousands of

other Christian Victorian families, the Caudles attend church together on Sunday morning; but Mrs. Caudle's chief concern, however, is for neither the sermon nor Christian love, but "how the
children looked at church to-day—like nobody else's children."
The Briggs's girls in their new chips looked down their respectable noses at the six little Caudles. Mrs. Caudle feels so strongly
about this rebuff that she declares that their own "children shall
not cross the threshold next Sunday, if they haven't things for the
summer." Respectability takes precedence over family prayer in
the Caudle household.

It is never mentioned whether Job reads aloud to his family, but
it is stated that he reads Milton's *Paradise Lost* to himself in bed.
Margaret's concept of marriage is outraged by this bold act: "If
that isn't insulting a wife to bring a book to bed, I don't know
what wedlock is." Job's choice of reading matter and his decision
to read in bed both shatter the image of family unity and ethereal
marital love. Moreover, when the time comes for their annual holiday at the seaside, there is again disunity, for they leave their six
children at home and travel to Margate and France by themselves. Instead of enjoying her vacation, Mrs. Caudle grows weary
both of the seashore and of Paris, and longs to return home.

Mrs. Caudle once referred to her home in London as "our dear
—dear home." In every respect, this home is the comic opposite of
Patmore's, Ruskin's, and Mrs. Ellis' picture of domestic bliss.
When Mr. Caudle comes home from the anxieties of his job as
tradesman, he finds no "place of peace"; on the contrary, his business life is more peaceful: Mrs. Caudle "knew that her husband
was too much distracted by his business as toyman and doll
merchant to digest her lessons in broad day." Her lectures are like
a parody of the Ellis manuals; indeed, Mrs. Caudle is at every
turn the opposite of Mrs. Ellis' good wife: she reinforces materialistic interests in Job's mind by arguing over domestic finances and
by urging him to find a wealthy godfather for the new baby.
Rather than advance his moral stature, she uses him to smuggle
French lace past customs. "Low anxieties and vulgar cares" are
her forte, and she would not dream of raising "the tone of his
mind" above them.

Quite naturally, Job flies from his home whenever possible; and
he spends his only peaceful moments in a tavern with Harry
Prettyman or with his friends at the Skylark Club. Even the name

of that group suggests that its members would fly from the household cage in order to enjoy common fellowship. Mrs. Ellis also discusses the man who likes to go out in the evening without his wife: "The rational woman, whose conversation on this occasion is to serve her purpose more effectively than tears, knows better than to speak of what her husband would probably consider a most unreasonable subject of complaint." She then advises the wife how to engage her husband in lively conversation until he looks at his watch, sees it is too late to join his companions, and "wonders whether any other man has a wife so delightful and entertaining as his own." [74]

Mrs. Caudle, however, is the *irrational* woman who speaks endlessly on what she *knows* her husband considers an unreasonable subject of complaint. She asks a rhetorical question which, in different particulars, reappears throughout the lectures: "How any man can leave his own happy fireside to go and sit and smoke, and drink, and talk with people who wouldn't one of 'em lift a finger to save him from hanging . . ." (7). The whole portrait of the Caudles appears to be a satiric caricature of the husband and wife who exist in the popular manuals of Mrs. Ellis, where a wife is a "cheering light" with a "softening, healing, harmonizing power . . . a being *to come home to,* in the happiest sense of that expression." [75]

Despite Job's being henpecked, he does possess principles which he refuses to compromise: he will not allow his mother-in-law to live with them, he does not reveal his Masonic secrets, and he continues to stay out with his friends and to smoke. Mrs. Caudle, however, is the real master of the home; for it is she who wins the major decisions: she refuses him a key to his own house, and she decides how much money is to be spent on the children's clothing, that washing is cheaper at home, that their wedding anniversary must be celebrated, that they vacation at Margate and then go to France, that they purchase a cottage in the country and call it the "Turtle-Dovery." Her iron rule might be contrasted with one historian's portrait of the typical Victorian wife: "Her attitude towards her husband, whom perhaps she would still address as 'Mr.,' was one of uncomfortable awe; . . . he was all-powerful, at least in the home. Of his business and his income she knew nothing. He regulated her life absolutely." [76]

The only thing in common in the two portraits is that Mrs.

Caudle usually addresses Job as "Mr. Caudle." Mrs. Caudle
wanted her family to rise in the social scale, which meant that a
certain amount of money was necessary as a prerequisite to respectability. She therefore made it her business to know a great
deal about her husband's finances. When he had become a direc-
tor of the Eel-Pie Island Railway, she explains that she opposes
his investment not because she dislikes money, but because "I like
it when I'm certain of it; no risks for me." She is so conversant
with his business transactions that she can recite verbatim entire
slogans used by the Eel-Pie Island speculators to advance their
stock. A cartoon in *Punch* called "The Momentous Question,"
which appeared a few weeks after the railway lecture, humorously parallels it. It shows Prince Albert sitting with his head
buried shamefully in his hand as his wife asks: "Tell me, oh tell
me, dearest Albert, have *you* any railway shares?" [77]

In the middle class, the commercial spirit was closely allied to
the passion for respectability. Its members strove to obtain respect
that money could then command even before the economic luxu-
ries that had previously lain beyond their reach. Money alone
clearly was not enough: one had to be a gentleman or a lady;
therefore, the rising middle class was eager to push or buy its way
into the upper class. After making money through trade, they
turned their children toward professions; dissent was rejected for
the Church of England; a gig, a country home, and even a title
were required for solid respectability. Their desires are represented in literature by such diverse characters as Mrs. Primrose in
Oliver Goldsmith's *The Vicar of Wakefield* (1766) and Alton
Locke's uncle in Charles Kingsley's *Alton Locke* (1850). The Victorians did not, of course, invent respectability; they merely inherited and perfected it as a social ideal.

Like Mr. Primrose, Job is opposed to his wife's social climbing.
Mrs. Caudle argues against his going to a tavern because it ruins
his image as a "respectable tradesman": "Your business is sure to
fall off; for what respectable people will buy toys for their children of a drunkard?" She reproves him for his sense of humor: "I
never heard any good come to a man who cared about jokes. No
respectable tradesman does." A constant complaint, suggestive of
Jane Austen's Mrs. Bennet in *Pride and Prejudice,* is that her children are "never dressed like other people's children." She places
respectability before charity when she rebukes Job for bailing

Prettyman out: "You should have shown yourself a respectable
man, and have let him been sent to prison." When Job refuses to
have the usurer Goldman for his sixth's child's godfather, Mrs.
Caudle calls him "a man of low notions" and prays that her sons
will learn to respect wealthy people more than their father does.
Carlyle has summed up Mrs. Caudle's pretensions in the term
"gigmanity."

Her notions of gentility continue to grow throughout the lectures until she finally concludes that "delicate health comes with
money" and that they must therefore seek a house in the country.
She suggests Brixton or Baalam Hill because "there, nobody visits
nobody, unless they're somebody." When Job rejects these
choices, she suggests Clapham Common, with the echoed response: "What! *The retired wholesales never visit* the retired re-
tails at Clapham? Ha! that's only your old sneering at the world,
Mr. Caudle; but I don't believe it. And after all, people should
keep to their station, or what was this life made for? Suppose a
tallow-merchant does keep himself above a tallow-chandler,—I
call it only a proper pride. What? *You call it the aristocracy of
fat?*" (75–76).

Mrs. Caudle's naming her country cottage the "Turtle-Dovery"
discloses an aspect of her philosophy of rhetoric: "In this world,
Mr. Caudle, names are sometimes quite as good as things." Her
last request is "a sweet little carriage, with our arms beautifully
painted on the panels." Mr. Caudle uses the occasion to make a
couple of jokes, first by suggesting her family's arms as "a mangle
in a stone-kitchen proper" and then by asking if she does not want
the family legs along with the arms. This last joke leads Mrs.
Caudle to warn him: "Don't be vulgar, Mr. Caudle. You might,
perhaps, talk in that way before you'd money in the Bank . . ."
(79–80). Needless to say, she gets her gig. The only extravagance
which Job forbids is her dressing their servant boy in livery to
appear with the gig at church on Sunday.

It is likely that Jerrold had Mrs. Ellis' condemnation of respectability in mind when he drew Mrs. Caudle: "I appeal to society
at large, whether the importance we many of us attach to appear-
ing well before the world, in other words, to dressing and living in
a certain style, has not irritated more tempers, destroyed more
peace, occasioned more disputes, broken more spirits, crossed
more love, hindered more improvement, and caused more spirit-

ual declension, than any other single cause which could be named." [78] Despite the accuracy of the diagnosis, one feels sure that the Caudles would be the last ones to recognize themselves as a case in point. Somehow they have not only complemented and survived each other but have managed somewhere among the verbal nightmares to bring forth six bright little Caudles. It is strangely easy to answer in the affirmative Mrs. Caudle's quiet question to Job: "Still we've been very happy, haven't we, Caudle?"

Mrs. Caudle's death greatly affected readers of *Punch*. In Thackeray's words, "though Mrs. Caudle had her faults, perhaps there was no woman who died more universally lamented than she. The want of her weekly discourse was felt over the kingdom." [79] At the end of the last installment of the *Curtain Lectures*, there was a note to the effect that other "Caudle Papers" are extant that reveal "what an aggravating man Caudle really was" and that these might appear in the next volume. Jerrold had obviously conceived of *Mr. Caudle's Breakfast Talk* before the *Curtain Lectures* ran out in order to lessen the disappointment his readers received at their conclusion. Therefore, in *Punch's Almanac* for 1846 one finds Mr. Caudle married to Miss Prettyman. Thackeray best summarizes contemporary feeling about the recent marriage when he writes that "it seems a wrong to the departed woman. We feel personally angry that her memory should be so slighted. . . ." [80]

The public was naturally unsatisfied with the *Almanac*. Compared to Mrs. Caudle, Job's character was flat; and his metamorphosis into a tyrant was too sudden to be convincing. The whole twelve chapters read like a parody of the *Curtain Lectures*, but there was nothing intrinsically funny about a husband's tyrannizing over his wife. Literary tradition and convention simply do not recognize this turn about as fair play. Consequently, Job's complaints over Sarah's poor cup of tea and her want of sympathy seem petty, unmanly, and unfunny. Nevertheless, there is a reasonably convincing motivation that gradually emerges to sustain the lectures, and that is Job's repressed hatred of his departed wife and his guilty conscience for having married Sarah Prettyman, since Mrs. Caudle begged him not to marry her after she died. He constantly compares Sarah to that "blessed woman" and says she is not fit to have stirred her tea. "I deserved to lose her," declares

Job. So, while his sentimental idealization of Margaret conceals Job's true feelings, his brutalization of Sarah reveals them. The undercurrent of this psychological duplicity assuredly was felt by readers who would not tolerate abuse of a woman they had come to love.

VI *Punch's Letters to His Son*

Published in *Punch* during 1842, *Punch's Letters to His Son* was Jerrold's first serial; and it proved to be highly successful. The letters are full of worldly wisdom satirically related through parables, stories, and examples, with topics that range from "The Advantages of being 'Nothing'" to "The Choice and Treatment of a Wife." Political, social, and moral problems of the time are satirized, and the whole serial constitutes a parody of *Lord Chesterfield's Letters to His Son.*

The educational theme is set forth by Mr. Punch: "I have sought to paint men as they are—to sketch the scenes of the world as they have presented themselves to my observation—to show the spring of human motives—to exhibit to the opening mind of youth the vulgar wires that, because unseen, make a mystery of common-place." [81] In short, each letter is aimed to teach his son how to get ahead in life through devious means or, in Mr. Punch's phrase, "how to secure the best cut of the shoulder."

In true eighteenth-century fashion, Jerrold begins with a dedication to the Lord Chamberlain, whom he compares to a pig before whom he will cast his pearls of wisdom as contained in the letters. His hostility is explained by the Lord Chamberlain's job of licensing plays, which Jerrold considered the death blow to legitimate drama; but, as Mr. Punch, he is free: "I pitch my tent wheresoever I will, in Westminster or not, without your warrant: I act my plays without your license" (3).

The introduction reveals that Punch's son is dead: "Yes, mutton was his fate." He was hanged in Newgate for having stolen a South-down wether. His fate is perhaps the best introduction to the nature of the letters as a satire of paternal advice and in particular of Chesterfield's inability to mold his son for a distinguished diplomatic career. Chesterfield's central theme in the letters was the necessity of acquiring perfect manners and of learning how to please as prerequisites for success in diplomacy. Jerrold parodies this theme by having Mr. Punch teach his son how to deceive others as a prerequisite to becoming "Nothing"—that is, being in a position "ready to accommodate yourself to any profitable circumstance that may present itself" (21).

Chesterfield counsels cleanliness: "In your person you must be accurately clean. . . ."[82] Mr. Punch, however, declares that "there is a fine natural religion in dirt" and advises his son to marry a dirty woman. Mr. Punch's second letter pokes fun at Chesterfield's advice to his son when he was studying with Mr. Maittaire. Chesterfield usually opened those letters with "I am very pleased with your last letter," indicating that his son was progressing well in his study of language. Mr. Punch also writes "I am much pleased with your last letter" and congratulates him on his linguistic progress under Dr. Birchbud; but, whereas Chesterfield would then demand that his son adhere to exact usage and grammar, Mr. Punch warns not to look "too closely into the significance and meaning of words." He teaches him that words were merely "counters that people play with" (11–12). It is only when his son is much older that Chesterfield tells him that words do not always convey their meaning, especially in conventional greetings and necessary flatteries; but Mr. Punch is taking his son beyond manners and is introducing him to the rhetoric of downright deception. He tells him not to question the words but to respect the power behind them, and he gives the example of men beheaded for questioning the meaning of "Dieu et mon droit."

Sometimes Chesterfield's advice is wily and worldly enough to need only the slightest turn to parody it: "Search . . . with the greatest care, into the characters of all those whom you converse with; endeavour to discover their predominant passions, their prevailing weaknesses, their vanities, their follies, and their humours. . . . This is the true knowledge of the world . . ." (CLS, 100). Mr. Punch's advice closely parallels this as he tells his son that, if he would learn of this world, he must forego foreign travel and instead "Plunge into the heart of a man. There you will find deserts, poisonous weeds, snakes, and a host of iniquities arrayed against a host. . . . Learn every nook of these; catalogue every object. It is in such spots you are to drive a prosperous trade; it is such articles you are to use in barter" (16). Mr. Punch pushes Chesterfield's advice to the perniciously pragmatic extreme that enables his son to become "a scholar in the weaknesses of the human heart" in order to manipulate people who stand in his way.

On the subject of lying, Chesterfield declares, "I really know nothing more criminal, more mean, and more ridiculous than lying"; and he counsels his son "that nothing but strict truth can carry you through the world" (*CLS*, 100). Like Chesterfield, who in many of his letters stresses the value of form and appearance, Mr. Punch tells his son to "take heed that you obtain not the evil reputation of a liar." But this apparently noble advice is only a prelude to advising outright duplicity: "What I wish to impress upon you, is the necessity of so uttering your verbal coinage, that to the superficial eye and careless ear, it may have all the appearance, all the ring of the true article. Herein lies the great wisdom of life" (35–36). Besides parodying Chesterfield's noble advice on truthfulness, Jerrold is also satirizing his double-dealing on this subject when, in a later letter, the Earl qualifies what he wrote earlier about lying: "Whereas, concealing the truth upon proper occasions, is as prudent and as innocent, as telling a lie upon any occasion, is infamous and foolish" (*CLS*, 195).

Mr. Punch describes to his son how learning may be obtained with the most economical use of time: "You shave once a day. Well, tear off a leaf of Blackstone, and whilst you are stropping your razor, carefully read it. This is so much time saved; and by this daily practice, you will in due season digest the whole of the Commentaries." Jerrold footnoted this passage: "Punch confesses that he owes the idea of this process to the Earl of Chesterfield, who in his Letter CI [CXXXIII, 106, in edition used here] to his son, suggests even a more ingenious mode of absorbing the essence of 'all the Latin Poets' " (50). There is a reason why Jerrold calls attention to Chesterfield here and not elsewhere. In other instances, his satire is obvious; but here he has cleaned up for his parody an anecdote that readers of *Punch* would consider vulgar and indecent. Mr. Punch's advice to learn while shaving is intended to conjure up Chesterfield's example of a man "who was so good a manager of his time, that he would not even lose that portion of it which the calls of nature obliged him to pass in the necessary-house; but gradually went through all the Latin Poets in those moments" (*CLS*, 106). After he tore the pages out and studied them, he "sent them down as a sacrifice to Cloacina." Thus Jerrold could elicit a laugh from his well-informed readers through a suggested vulgarity and still remain innocent of any indecency himself.

Chesterfield cautions his son in his choice of friends: "Endeavour as much as you can to keep company with people above you. There you rise, as much as you sink with people below you. . . . Do not mistake when I say company above you, and think I mean with regard to their birth; that is the least consideration; but I mean with regard to their merit, and the light in which the world considers them" (*CLS*, 101). Mr. Punch begins his advice on an equally lofty plane by quoting Chesterfield's remark that "whatever is worth *doing* at all, is worth *doing well*" and then applying the axiom to the treatment of a friend: "it is to defeat the purpose of all friendship . . . to ally yourself with any companion, who cannot better your fortunes: to whom you cannot on all occasions resort . . . for what must be indisputably acceded to be the purest, the noblest offering of a human soul,—ready money" (59). Chesterfield's advice is really not so far removed from Mr. Punch's on general principles: both suggest that the way to get ahead is to choose one's friends carefully, making sure they are in a position to help one advance in society. By reducing merit to the material level of "ready money," Jerrold makes the general principle suddenly seem pernicious.

Chesterfield, who stresses the importance of flattery in learning how to please, states that men "are most and best flattered upon those points where they wish to excel, and yet are doubtful whether they do or not" (*CLS*, 102–3). Jerrold, who places both political and social flattery in the category of hypocrisy, refuses to accept Chesterfield's distinction between necessary flattery and "abject and criminal flattery." He ridicules the Earl's advice by presenting a satirically sophistical argument on behalf of "wisdom and intellect":

Your patron is an ass: you hear his braying—you see his ears: *asinus* is written all over him in Nature's boldest round-hand. Well, by delicately dwelling upon the melodious wisdom of his words—by adroitly touching on the intellectual beauty with which fate has endowed him, you make him for the time love wisdom because he thinks it a part of himself—you draw his admiration towards the expression of the intellectual every time he looks in a mirror. You are thus, in an indirect way, serving the cause of wisdom and intellect by juggling a fool into a worshipper. (66)

Since Chesterfield had early become addicted to gambling, he took especial care to warn his son that the vice "draws you into a thousand scrapes, leaves you penniless, and gives you the airs and manners of an outrageous madman. . . ." He also warns that drinking is "equally destructive to body and mind" (*CLS*, 95). Jerrold cynically gives Mr. Punch the words of an approving libertine; "Depend upon it, the bottle is the spring, the true source of all human inspiration—the fountain from which all philosophers, all sages, have drunk their best wisdom." In order to remain consistent with the theme of hypocrisy and sham that runs through all the letters, Mr. Punch tells his son when he is in society "to maintain the look and something of the reasoning powers of a man" even though "your whole carcass is throbbing with alcohol." On the subject of gambling, Jerrold parodies a line from Pope: "Gaming is a moral Aaron's rod, and swallows up all meaner passions." He advises it as an open and "generous mode of living upon men" and declares "the true jewels of life . . . are the four aces" (71–74).

Jerrold has converted Chesterfield's "course of polite education" into an art of hypocrisy offered not only as a parody but as a criticism of moral principles in Victorian society. Of all Victorian attitudes none was so often attacked by the Victorians themselves as hypocrisy. Carlyle, John Stuart Mill, Thackeray, Dickens, James Anthony Froude, and John Morley led the major crusade against this vice, but Jerrold made a small but revealing contribution towards understanding prevalent attitudes toward sham and humbug.

Exploiting the idea of the first serial, Jerrold published *Punch's Complete Letter Writer* two years later. Although it enjoyed a great success, the satire lacked a central point of view, being made up of letters to and from all manner of people from meddling maiden aunts advising their nieces against marriage to heartless landlords extorting their monthly rents from innocent laborers. The replies to these letters are often written to a confidant, and illustrate that there are two sides to every story; nevertheless, Jerrold's sympathies clearly lie with the victims of injustice and tyranny.

VII *Female Crusoe*

The transition from Jerrold's world to the present age is made
easy in his serial entitled *The Life and Adventures of Miss Robinson Crusoe,* since it is based upon a book known and enjoyed by
all. Women have always been a vulnerable target for satirists, but
Victorian ladies seem more vulnerable than any other group because of their unique place in social history. In Jerrold's serial, one
finds a microcosm in the form of a desert island where the Victorian young woman, replete with her ambitions, vanities, accomplishments, and frustrations, engages sympathy and laughter.

The *Life and Adventures of Miss Robinson Crusoe*[83] not only
burlesques Daniel Defoe but satirizes finishing schools, marriageable young ladies, contemporary fashions, and vain women. Since
Defoe's Crusoe spends the greater part of his time setting up
house and establishing a domestic routine, Miss Crusoe is an especially well-chosen protagonist for the burlesque. Like her ances-
tor, Miss Crusoe tells the story in diary form. She also comes from
middle-class parents and fails to heed her father's advice to remain content "in the middle state of life." She has romantic visions
of marrying a rajah in India. Although her father promises her a
"steady and sober husband," he has spent most of his money in
dowries for her two married sisters. Nevertheless, his promise
continues to haunt her with regret throughout her narrative; and
her situation corresponds to the regret Defoe's Crusoe experiences
for not listening to his father about the advantages of the middle
state of life. Whereas Defoe establishes Crusoe's self-reliance by
showing him as overcoming many perils at sea, Jerrold deliberately establishes his heroine as a completely dependent, uneman-
cipated woman. The only preparation for her forthcoming adventures comes from the Blackheath finishing school: she could play
six tunes upon a grand piano, dance, sing, and speak some Italian.

Jerrold parodies Defoe's matter-of-fact style that revels in long
lists of facts or catalogues of material objects. Before Miss Crusoe
departs for India, she buys "six dozen of double-scented lavender,
a dozen of the finest milk of roses, twenty pounds of the best pearl
powder, a gross of court-plaster, six ounces of musk, a quart of oil
of bergamotte, two boxes of rouge, and—not to weary the reader
—a hundred of the like articles indispensable to a young gentle-
woman" (214). Just as tradesmen might have rejoiced in Defoe's

economics and compilations of material goods, so women (and Miss Crusoe states that she is writing for them alone) must have enjoyed hearing the familiar names of cosmetics and other fashionable items mentioned throughout the serial, which allowed them to identify themselves more easily with Miss Crusoe on her otherwise fantastic journey.

Miss Crusoe's ruling passion is vanity, and her wardrobe plays a major role in supporting it. Jerrold humorously attempts to enter the female mind by making the reader see and hear things through a woman's peculiar affections and associations. When Captain Biscuit orders, "put the ship in stays," Miss Crusoe forces herself to look as grave as the rest of the passengers, but secretly thinks the Captain is a great wit. When the ship finally sinks in a storm, Miss Crusoe is miraculously supported by her garments on the waves, swims toward shore (a skill, she explains, learned at Margate, not at Blackheath), and is safely anchored to the coastal rocks by her flounces. Fashion has seldom been influenced by practicality, and the crinoline became popular at a time when women were beginning to travel more than they had ever done before. *Punch* had numerous cartoons showing crinolined ladies trying to board omnibuses or being stuck in the doorway of a railway carriage. Jerrold's satire suggests that the full dress with its embroidery has it practicality—at least in fiction. These clothes humorously expedite the story, considering it took Defoe two pages to get his hero through battling the waves, holding his breath, and grasping rocks before he safely landed on the shore.

Jerrold closely follows Defoe's narrative, but he intersperses sudden incongruities to highlight women's vanity. Crusoe's first concerns are hunger and fear of being devoured by wild beasts. Miss Crusoe gives a token acknowledgement to similar problems, but her real fear was "lest some savage should see me in my horrible *déshabille*." When Crusoe returns to the shipwreck, the first thing he lowers onto his raft is food, then clothes, tools, and arms. He gathers up the clothes hurriedly because "I had other things which my eye was more upon, as first, tools to work with on shore." [84] Jerrold, however, changes the order to clothes, food, medicine and weapons. One of Miss Crusoe's chief delights is rummaging among the clothes of the dead women passengers and discovering "the many falsehoods made of buckram, and wool, and wadding." Again, Jerrold counted on the innate curiosity of women readers, who naturally were interested in other women's clothes, to overcome the grim aspects of such rummaging. His readers could vicariously help break open the boxes to be dazzled by canary-colored satin slips, French slippers, and plum-colored silk. Jerrold, who considered Crusoe's rooting through the ship's goods as the special province of women, has Miss Crusoe exclaim, "who, when she likes, *can* rummage like a woman?" (225, 227).

The desolate island serves as a testing ground for the worth of English finishing schools. The six tunes Miss Crusoe can play on a grand piano, her needlework, and her Italian are to no avail; even the geography she learned cannot help her to locate the island: "I had been taught to talk about California and Behring's Straits, and the Euxine and Patagonia, as if they were all so many old acquaintances; and yet I knew not if at that moment I might not be upon some of them" (232). Jerrold's satire here may not at first be clear since one would expect the girl's geography lessons to be the most helpful of all in her present dilemma. Jerrold assumes the reader is familiar with the mechanical techniques of teaching geography that left the student with a stock of answers to standardized and often trivial questions. Girls were subjected to Mangnall's *Historical and Miscellaneous Questions for the Use of Young People* and to Mrs. R. Ward's *The Child's Guide to Knowledge*. A typical question and answer from Mrs. Ward's book is: "Q. What is sago? A. The inner pith of a species of palm-tree growing in the Moluccas and Ceram." [85] There was no attempt to make the child think for herself; everything was learned by rote. This method of teaching began in the home and was continued by governesses and those who kept boarding schools. Despite the levity of the satire, Jerrold is pointing out a serious failing in the education of women.

The island also serves as a device by which Jerrold can satirize respectability. Miss Crusoe longs for an "essential something," namely, the *Morning Post*, since it used to allow her "to catch the odour of high society." Later she finds some silver forks aboard ship; and, because it was "one of the first principles" of her education "to consider a silver fork essential to any assertion soever of human dignity," she feels herself "lifted by the discovery." The status symbol of fine silverware was very important to the middle class, and this interest contributed earlier to the nickname of a literary genre, "the silver-fork novels."

Crusoe made notches in a post to mark the days and a special mark for the Sabbath. Jerrold portrays Miss Crusoe as a civilized heathen who uses the frame of a looking glass for her calendar, in which she cuts "double notches for what I recollected were opera nights." The opera, of course, had the greatest appeal to members of the rising middle class because attending allowed them to arrive in fine carriages, employ their fans, display their best manners, and feel themselves to be a vital part of the company of generals, dukes, and the royal family.

Jerrold continues to use his heroine's vanity as the central theme of his burlesque. Defoe's hero draws up a list of six evils that befell him, which he balances with six corresponding goods. Jerrold parodies the first two entries, which in Defoe's version read:

Evil	Good
I am cast upon a horrible desolate island, void of all hope of recovery.	But I am alive, and not drowned, as all my ship's company was.
I am singled out and separated, as it were, from all the world to be miserable.	But I am singled out, too, from all the ship's crew to be spared from death; and He that miraculously saved me from death can deliver me from this condition.

(RC, 73)

Jerrold adapts this method to the female mind:

Evil	Good
I am thrown upon a desolate island, without a blessed soul to speak to.	Then I have this consolation— There's nobody to scandalise me.
I am singled out to be a single women, when I might have been a wife and a parent.	I might have been married early to a brute, and been a grandmother at eight-and-thirty!

(250)

Whereas Defoe limits the vision of island life by presenting it from the point of view of a trueborn Englishman, Jerrold absurdly narrows the field by forcing his reader to see through the eyes of a girl who sees life through the eyes of the *Morning Post.* Crusoe's

list presents a cogent, reasonable argument against despair; Miss
Crusoe not only foregoes any religious consideration but completely rationalizes her condition. The whole purpose of her trip
was to secure a husband. Since Miss Crusoe's guiding force is vanity, she is made to suffer more than her self-reliant literary ances-
tor, who can exist without mirrors and the eyes of society. By
removing such necessary reflectors from Miss Crusoe, Jerrold suggests that the vain, social-minded, middle-class young lady no
longer has a real existence. Crusoe can create a little England out
of his inner resources; Miss Crusoe can only print with a stick
upon the sand the words *Morning Post* and watch as the rising
tide "would wash that morning print away!"

Nevertheless, Miss Crusoe's need to see herself drives her to
burnish the bottom of a frying pan. When she can see the tip of
her nose, she begins to feel the blessings of civilization return.
Like Defoe's hero, she does not succumb to nature but triumphs
over it; she constantly strives to reconstruct polite society, and her
crowning success comes after she rescues her girl Friday from the
cannibals and makes her into a lady's maid: "For I thought to
myself, 'Now I no longer need make my own fire, and can hence-
forth have my breakfast in bed.'" Jerrold, who hated slavery as
well as the mistreatment suffered by many domestic servants, satirizes Defoe's hero, who teaches Friday to say "Master" before
re-educating him; and he attacks the upper middle class who follow the "great principle" of Miss Crusoe's genteel mother: "servants could not . . . be kept 'too much under.' . . ."

Crusoe attempts to teach Friday the principles of Christianity,
but Miss Crusoe models her servant on different lines: "I insisted
that she should submit to wear . . . stays." The details of this
painful episode are aimed to excite the sympathy of all female
readers: "At length, however, the stays were on, and I prepared
myself to lace them. I knew that by doing this I was teaching the
first lesson in civilisation, and felt myself strengthened for the task
accordingly. But shall I ever forget the screams of Friday, as I
laced hole after hole? . . . the more Friday screamed, the tighter
I laced, till, in the end, her figure was so unlike vulgar nature, it
almost approached perfection" (266). Tight lacing was in vogue
during the 1840's because the amount of underclothing women
wore was so great that, without a corset, they would have had a
thirty-inch waist line to their dresses. The subject of tight lacing

raged through the newspapers and magazines of the 1840's and 1850's, and frightening books were also published on the subject, such as William Coulson's *Deformities of the Chest and Spine.* Miss Crusoe's "first lesson in civilisation" not only ridicules a current mode of fashion but suggests, through a humorous metaphor, the painful and absurd consequences of one nation's attempt to reshape another race or country according to its own standards. According to Jerrold's metaphor, Friday will approach perfection when she is least like herself ("vulgar nature"—India) and most like Crusoe ("perfection"—England).

Keeping in mind that Miss Crusoe suffered greatly from not having been taught to cook (she managed to kill a wild turkey, but it is uneaten throughout the story because she could only "work a peacock in worsted"), Jerrold created *Capsicum House for Young Ladies* in the following year to save future Miss Crusoes from a similar fate.

VIII   *The Education of Young Ladies*

Capsicum House for Young Ladies is only one of a number of burlesques that appeared in 1847 on the subject of feminine education. About two months before Jerrold's serial began, Thackeray had poked fun at girls' boarding schools in the first part of *Vanity Fair.* Tennyson's topical medley *The Princess* humorously and seriously describes a woman's college that offers a radically new curriculum, suggestive of Queen's College that opened a year later. And the large sale of Mrs. Hugo Reid's book, *A Plea for Women* (1843), is indicative of the public's interest in the question of female education. She argues that women's intellectual development should take priority over feminine "accomplishments." Numerous articles began to appear in the various journals demanding the improved educational status of women that would put them on a more equal basis with men.

Since the educational question was bound up with the problem of women's freedom to work for a living, there were, however, few immediate improvements. Parents either had their daughters educated at home or sent them away after the age of twelve to boarding schools. At these establishments the feminine virtues— together with a smattering of religion, geography, sewing, music, dancing, and penmanship—were acquired as polite prerequisites for the marriage market. Thackeray's Miss Pinkerton's Academy

in *Vanity Fair* captures the essence of these schools, and Amelia
Sedley is a typical, finished young lady: she is industrious, obedient, sweet-tempered, and has a deportment and carriage "so
requisite for every young lady of fashion." [86] Graduates who failed
to capture a husband usually had the grim alternative of becoming governesses.

Miss Bianca Griffin, who runs Capsicum House, has invited Mr.
Punch as a guest observer to her school. By 1847, Jerrold had
become so closely identified with the persona of Mr. Punch that,
at the end of the first chapter, Leech caricatures him as Mr. Punch
greeting Miss Griffin and Miss Fluke, one of her students. For the
rest of the illustrations, Leech returned to his conventional portrait of Mr. Punch, whose resemblance to Jerrold is more remote.

Jerrold states at the outset that "Miss Griffin's establishment is
really finishing, its whole object being to turn out the fair pupils
fully impressed with the solemn responsibilities of marriage.
. . ." [87] Although the object of Capsicum House is conventional
enough, Miss Griffin's "private and confidential" Prospectus reveals a unique method of education, based upon the principles of
the "Griffinian System." Jerrold has invented this system to satirize
the cries for the emancipation of women by giving the prospectus
an eloquent and rhetorical turn:

> But the Emancipation of the Female Mind is at hand. It cannot be
> doubted that, in an age that has given us the Electric Telegraph and
> the Benevolent Oblivion of Ether, it cannot—Miss G. fearlessly ob-
> serves—be doubted that the Female Mind will burst from the thraldom
> that has too long dwarfed it to the dimension of her Master. The Grif-
> finian System is the great discovery that will effect this moral revolu-
> tion, elevating Woman to a pinnacle that even the most hopeful
> scarcely dare raise their eyes to. (146)

Jerrold believed that the education of women as men's equals
would be premature as long as society withheld jobs and political
rights from them. His advice to women was conservative: "Learn
and practice your duties; and as for your rights, why, leave them
to come as best they may." Jerrold respected the rights of women
and even fought, as has been noted, for their acceptance into his
Whittington Club, but he remained characteristically opposed to
any large-scale radical social upheavals.

Although the language of the prospectus sounds like an ultimatum for women's intellectual education ("Education is the great lever that will lift Woman into her proper place"), it turns out that Miss Griffin wants "the Education, not of the Mind, but the Feelings" (147). Jerrold avoids the more serious theme undertaken by Tennyson in *The Princess,* although he goes beyond Thackeray's Miss Pinkerton's conventional academy by presenting a boarding school that absurdly promises to emancipate the female mind. Capsicum House, then, stands somewhere between the two: its daily routine burlesques conventional boarding schools and its prospectus ridicules the radical demands for women's educational rights. Jerrold's conservative point of view is closer, therefore, to Ruskin's than to Mill's. Ruskin advocated an improvement over the boarding-school education, but he was unwilling to go as far as some of his contemporaries. He thought knowledge should confirm the female mind's "natural instincts of justice, and refine its natural tact of love," and help her to understand and aid the work of men.[88] Mill, on the other hand, in his essay, *On the Subjection of Women,* argued that the principles of liberty and representation were as applicable to women as to men.

The practical goal of the Griffinian System is for a girl to "become the Master of Man" through culinary conquest: "The weapons to subdue Man are not to be found in the library, but in the kitchen!!" Miss Griffin views all men as ruled by the passion of selfishness, which is amenable to good cooking: "Like a trout, so to speak, he must be tickled to be taken." She discredits the standard finishing school because it teaches useless accomplishments: "the Finished Young Lady can paint a peacock on velvet, she has so light a touch. But can she tell the age of a simple fowl at the poulterers?" It gradually becomes clear why the school is called "Capsicum," since it purports to season young girls into cunning wives, or in Miss Griffin's garbled Wordsworth, "the girl is mother of the wife!" (147–55).

The cooking classes and examinations are carefully observed by Mr. Punch. The girls cultivate the herbs themselves in order to learn stuffing "from first principles." There is also a marriage-service class where the girls are taught to say "I will" with aplomb. This course is taught by Tamerlane Corks, formerly an actor at Drury Lane. Jerrold digresses in order to ridicule the notorious spectaculars that were dominating London theaters and

which often paraded live animals on stage: "However, it was not
for a man like Mr. Corks to associate with camels, and make companions of elephants; and, therefore, in a word, you see in my
friend Tamerlane the Decline of the Drama" (155, 164).

Miss Fluke, the bright but rebellious student, turns up in full
bridal dress "to do all honour to the tuition of Mr. Tamerlane
Corks." Indeed, she reappears throughout the story to ridicule the
Griffinian System by asserting her common sense. The emphasis
upon cooking is so pervasive that some students need reminding
of the distinction between food and marriage. Corks instructs
Miss Trimby: "you answer *'I will'* as though you were asked to
take a custard, and not a husband" (171, 179).

Jerrold's best satire is of Miss Griffin's futile attempts to incorporate realism into her system by hiring the drunkard Blossoms to
live on the grounds and come "home" late in order to prepare
students to enact "the Injured Wife." The scheme is comically un-
dermined by the students who fail to muster convincing wrath; by
the spinster instructor, Miss Carraways, who is infatuated with
Blossoms; by Miss Fluke, who indignantly declares, "Do you suppose when I'm married I shan't know how to scold my husband?
. . . You only find the husband, and I'll find the injuries"; and by
Mr. Blossoms himself, who confesses, "I'm too peaceable in my
liquor. If I could only remember to break a few windows, I should
begin to have hopes" (195, 190).

The last two chapters concern the example set by the successful
alumna Lady M'Thistle, who captured her husband with haggis
that conjured up in his imagination "his blue hills" and "the rush-
ing streams," and made him believe "his foot was upon the
heather!" She also appealed to his sense of economy by exhibiting
her frugal taste by wearing "fireflies captive in white muslin
bonds" instead of expensive jewelry. Before the serial closes, Miss
Fluke reveals that Miss Griffin has fallen in love with Tamerlane
and Miss Fluke's rebelliousness is pardoned because she possesses
"so much enthusiasm" (202, 201, 207).

Capsicum House's self-contained world is filled with illusion
and impracticality; the humor of the serial depends upon the im-
position of reality upon an absurd system or ideal world. As her
name suggests, Miss Fluke anchors Capsicum House to earth and
gives the lie to the Griffinian System as stated with a pun: "no
young woman's education can be thought complete, who has not

made, I may say it, a Cook's voyage round the globe." Gradually
the other characters begin to break out of the System: Miss Carraways succumbs to Mr. Blossoms; Miss Palmer cannot play the Injured Wife; and even Miss Griffin falls hopelessly in love with
Corks. The reality of love cannot be confined to a cook book or
contained within the insubstantial boundaries of Capsicum
House. This breakdown is not unlike the gradual one of absurd
rules and regulations in Shakespeare's *Love's Labours Lost* and in
Tennyson's *The Princess*.

It was suggested earlier that in the *Curtain Lectures* Jerrold
was satirizing the manuals of Sarah Ellis. In *Capsicum House*, he
alludes to her *Wives of England* more than once. Miss Palmer's
inability to overcome her innate innocence and sweet disposition
causes her to fail miserably as an Injured Wife, and Jerrold portrays her as a potentially perfect wife who would embody the
principles of the *Wives of England*. The last thing she does before
confronting Blossoms is to wink at the Ellis manual. Mrs. Ellis
believed that the correct attitude of the married woman was "one
of the trial of Principle rather than the fruition of Hope." [89] When
Miss Palmer approaches Blossoms, Jerrold exclaims, "Beautiful
are such trials, that is, most beautiful in their failure" (194). Beautiful though her failure to frown may be, Miss Carraways, the
voice of reality, interposes: "If you don't frown, and speak your
mind, you'll always be put upon."

The fault of marriage manuals, Jerrold seems to be saying, is
that they present a self-contained ideal world that is as far removed from real life as Capsicum House. The "piercing, cruel
thorns" that await Miss Palmer "in the worldly way" are indiffer-
ent to cook books, abstract virtues, and accomplishments. Miss
Fluke, who sees through all systems and abstractions, wisely exclaims to Palmer: "Oh, come away from this nonsense." On the
other hand, absurd as Capsicum House may be, Jerrold ranks it
above the conventional finishing school because at least it produces
good cooks.

CHAPTER 4

The Earnest Jester: Instructive Fiction

I Character Sketches

J ERROLD wrote no less than fifty character sketches that vary as widely in their range of subjects as in their methods of presentation. Although most of them follow the informal pattern established by such authors as Charles Lamb, Leigh Hunt, and William Hazlitt, Jerrold's sketches do not reveal his personal life. Jerrold's *Full-Lengths*, a group of character sketches drawn from everyday life and everyday people, which first appeared in the *Monthly Magazine* (1826), possibly served as models for Dickens' *Sketches by Boz*, that began to appear in the same magazine seven years later. Among Jerrold's characters are "The Greenwich Pensioner," "The Drill Sergeant," "The Tax-Gatherer," "The Jew Slop-Seller," and "The Ship's Clergyman," a grouping which reflects an interest in people and places similar to that of Dickens in his "Brokers and Marine-Store Shops" and in "The Hospital Patient."

Inspired by the success of "Boz" and influenced by the technique of Theodore Hook (*Sayings and Doings*), Jerrold returned to writing sketches of character in 1835, which he published in *Blackwood's Magazine*. These, with other sketches printed in the *New Monthly Magazine*, were later reprinted in a volume entitled *Men of Character*, which was illustrated by Thackeray. Each of the eight characters undergoes a number of experiences that dramatize his predominant trait, and all the action is structured to that end. Incidents and episodes have no artistic connection, and their extravagance is justified only by the hero's chief characteristic, which is indicated in the titles of the sketches: "Job Pippins: the Man 'Couldn't Help It,'" "Jack Runnymede: the Man of Many 'Thanks,'" "Adam Buff: the Man 'Without a Shirt,'" "Matthew Clear: the Man 'Who Saw His Way,'" "John Applejohn: the

Man Who 'Meant Well,' " "Barnaby Palms: the Man who 'Felt His Way,' " "Christopher Snub: Who was 'Born to be Hanged,' " and "Creso Quattrino: the Man 'Who Died Rich.' "

The peculiar form of the titles is most likely derived from Theodore Hook's *Sayings and Doings: or, Sketches From Life* (1824–28), which includes such stories as "The Man of Many Friends" and "Cousin William; or, the Fatal Attachment." Jerrold also follows Hook's technique, borrowed from the minor theater, of portraying characters by making their "doings" rigidly illustrate a "saying." Both men had before them the example of the farce stage, which had long exhibited characters with "humours."

An examination of "Job Pippins" reveals the similarity of Jerrold's sketches to the farce drama. Each of the episodes illustrates Jerrold's naturalistic theme that Job is "nothing more than the hero of accident, the plaything, and finally, the prosperous, man of chance." [1] Job, a barber in the household of Sir Scipio Mannikin, is one day called in to dress Lady Scipio's hair, in the process of which his passion mounts and he kisses her. The entire mansion goes into an uproar, and Job exclaims, "I—I—I—couldn't help it!" Jerrold breaks in, tongue-in-check, to corroborate his hero's veracity: "And Job Pippins could *not* help it."

Job heads for London but winds up at an ale house on the road because "Sally," the daughter, stood at the door of the inn, and—how could he help it?—Job entered." Here he meets Cuttles, the clerk from Job's parish, who has money which the parish ladies, who believe Job innocent, collected to help defray his court expenses against Sir Scipio. When Job tells Cuttles the true story, he leaves with the money; and the landlord calls Job a fool for telling the truth, but he replies that he "couldn't help it." Job's trip to London is full of improbable incidents: he meets Sir Scipio half dead from an accident, falls in with highwaymen who rob him, steals some clothes, and is the object of mistaken identity at a nearby lodge, catches the fancy of a rich widow with whom he escapes when his true identity is about to be revealed, marries her and goes on to live a decent, respectable, lucrative life.

The other seven sketches of character, like "Job Pippins," exploit characteristics of three genres—the character sketch, the short story, and the farcical drama. In Jerrold's own words, all of the characters run "into mere grotesque." They become caricatured allegories: Jack Runnymede is the fool of truth and patriotism amidst a corrupt society, who suddenly changes into a dishonest purser; Adam Buff succeeds in life because everyone mistakes his vanity for bravery: Matthew Clear lands in Newgate Prison because he lacks prudence and self-knowledge; John Applejohn's good intentions are consistently misinterpreted by a cynical society but he is ultimately rewarded by a good marriage; Barnaby Palms undergoes moral and physical destruction in the world of London because he lacked a father to prepare him for the encounter; Christopher Snub is a completely unredeemed rogue from birth whose crimes are ironically rewarded by a successful career in trade; and Creso Quattrino, who lives only for money, goes into debt and discovers his solvency just before he dies of the poison that he took to save his pride. All of these unbelievable characters have entered a moral world in which they do not belong; they are grotesque illustrations of virtues and vices that invite the applause of an audience accustomed to farce and melodrama.

Jerrold's next venture into writing character sketches was *Heads of the People* (1839), a series of "portraits of the English," written by Jerrold, Leigh Hunt, Thackeray, and others. Marked by social satire, sentiment, and wit, and by a return to the earlier informal style of his *Full Lengths,* Jerrold's contributions extended over a wide range of subjects: "The Pew Opener," "The Young Lord," "The Undertaker," "The Post Man," "The Ballad-Singer," "The Hangman," "The Linen-Draper's Assistant," "The Debtor and Creditor," "The 'Lion' of a Party," "The Cockney," "The Money-Lender," "The Diner-Out," "The Pawnbroker," and "The Printer's Devil." Most of the sketches are of types, rather than of individuals; and the types are primarily of professions or ways of life, rather than of virtues or vices, although the Undertaker and Shopkeeper represent a specific class of swindlers. An examination of "The Cockney" exemplifies Jerrold's technique.

Like the Greenwich Pensioner, whose war-scarred body is a monument of England's national greatness, the Cockney is a likable but proud fellow who believes he affords the best example of national virtue, cleverness, and wit. Whereas Jerrold has to interpret the Pensioner's wounds for him ("in his binded eye is Howe's Victory"), the Cockney is conscious of his own merit. The sketch begins with a brief account of the Cockney of the past when he was "invested with higher and more curious attributes than are awarded to him in these days." Years ago, when transportation to London was hard to come by, the Cockney struck visitors and rustics with "no passing wonderment" because they were unused to seeing anyone with "his dress, his air, his look of extraordinary wisdom." Now Jerrold declares, "the inventors of railways have much to answer for." Against the background of the past Jerrold projects the image of the contemporary Cockney; and he notes that, despite his lessened importance in the eyes of outsiders, "he himself remains, in his own assurance, the same clever, knowing, judicious, sprightly, witty fellow that he ever was." Since the Cockney is a unique creation of London, Jerrold employs familiar place names, buildings, statues, and ceremonies of that city to suggest his local character:

He was born and bred in Bishopsgate Within; and for that unanswerable reason, is in no way to be cozened. He is part and parcel of the greatest city upon earth; a piece of the very heart of the empire. The Mansion House, the Monument, and Guildhall, are all to him more ancient than the pyramids. Gog and Magog, to the real Cockney, stand in the remote relation of ancestors: he is wood of their wood. Politics to him are most familiar matters; he can discuss state questions as easily as he could play at push-pin; and displace a ministry with the same readiness as, in the days of his apprenticeship, he could take down the shutters.[2]

The passage then describes him as removing his hat as the Queen passes to Parliament, and the paragraph closes with a typical example of Jerrold's wit: "his mind hath no greater range than that of his shop; and his every thought, like every omnibus, runs to the Bank."

Having set the present-day Cockney against the one of former times, Jerrold notes a contrast between the middle-aged and the youthful varieties. In his more sportive season, "his animal spirits are so abundant that they, incontinently, make him knock off hats; deal body-blows; and send him playing leapfrog over the heads of his fellow revellers." The boisterous youth has its counterpart in the epicurean and self-satisfied wisdom of the older Cockney who enjoys his day away from the shop: "Sunday comes; and in a tavern bower, or humbler tea-garden, with one eye upon his pipe, and the other upon a bed of marigolds, the Cockney will sit and smoke, and smoke, and drink an unconsidered quantity of British

brandy; and satisfactorily consider his own virtues, complacently
taking for himself the very highest rank for true piety, and earnest, downright, Sabbath-Keeping, above all the other sinful nations of this sinful world." [3] Jerrold also illustrates, however, the
Cockney's behavior not only in London but abroad, since "he is
not to be thoroughly known when rooted to London soil." He is
depicted as "swelling with national greatness" after a sentry
chases him away from the statue of Diana in the Tuileries for
writing his name and address on her right leg so that future visitors of Paris may know he has been there.

The entire sketch is built upon a series of contrasts: the early
and contemporary Cockney, the young and middle-aged Cockney, and the Cockney in London and abroad. His timeless traits of
wit, pride, judiciousness, and sprightliness organize the contrasts
into one comprehensive image of the eternal Cockney who has in
him "infinite fun and humor."

In 1843, Jerrold introduced a new character named Peter Jenkins to readers of *Punch.* Although the Jenkins papers were not
planned as a serial they appeared frequently for over a year. Jenkins became so familiar to readers that Jerrold could allude to him
as late as 1848 and expect him to be recognized as the perfect
snob. Although Jenkins was originally created as a satiric personification of the *Morning Post,* he soon became more interesting as a
portrait of a snob than as a satiric weapon against the newspaper;
and, as such, he anticipates Thackeray's *Snobs of England* by
three years. It is very possible that Thackeray used Jenkins as the
prototype for his *Snob* papers, especially since he contributed a
few Jenkins numbers himself a year after Jerrold first conceived
the idea. For a time, it was even thought that Thackeray initiated
Punch's attacks upon the *Post* and that he wrote most of the Jenkins papers.

This mistaken assumption led to a humorous piece of injustice.
The original of Jenkins was Rumsey Forster, a *Morning Post* re-
porter, whose function it was to note down names as people en-
tered the drawing room for fashionable receptions. Believing that
Thackeray was the chief culprit behind the anonymous ridicule,
Forster waited several years, until Thackeray achieved fame and
was himself invited to fashionable soirées, to take his revenge.
Forster related his tactics to Henry Vizetelly:

"You should know, sir," he said solemnly, "that at Stafford House, Lady Palmerston's and the other swell places, a little table is set for me just outside the drawing-room doors, where I take down the names of the company as these are announced by the attendant footmen. Well, Mr. Thackeray was at the Marquis of Lansdowne's the other evening, and his name was called out as customary; nevertheless, I took very good care that it should not appear in the list of the company at Lansdowne House, given in the 'Post.' A night or two afterwards I was at Lord John Russell's, and Mr. Thackeray's name was again announced, and again I designedly neglected to write it down; whereupon the author of the 'Snobs of England,' of all persons in the world—bowed, and bending over me, said: 'Mr. Thackeray'; to which I replied: 'Yes, sir, I am quite aware'; nevertheless the great Mr. Thackeray's name did not appear in the 'Post' the following morning!" [4]

Jerrold introduced Jenkins in "The 'Post' at the Opera": "A wonderful creature has made his descent upon *The Morning Post!* It is not generally known, but this paragon of animals, who 'does' the Opera, is at the present moment a claimant for the long dormant title of Bletheranskate—yes, if he succeeds, the man now known as nothing more than Peter Jenkins, will be the Earl of Bletheranskate." [5] By making him an opera critic, Jerrold can use the opera house as a microcosm of England's aristocracy, from which vantage point Jenkins views all society: "He very properly looks upon the condition of Opera boxes as the barometer of 'society.' If Duchesses turn out in their best diamonds and sweetest smiles,—why, the weavers must be doing better at Bolton and Paisley. . . ." [6]

Jerrold's usual technique is to take actual passages from the *Morning Post,* credit them to Jenkins, and develop his character out of these quotations with his own satiric embellishments. For example, from the *Morning Post* for March 13, 1843, he quotes the preamble to a review of a performance of Donizetti's opera *Adelia* at Her Majesty's Theatre: "Ever since the Italian lyrical drama crossed the Alps in the suite of the tasteful Medicis, its vogue has daily increased, it has become a ruling passion—it is *the quintessence of all civilized pleasures,* and *wherever* its principal *virtuosi* hoist their standard, *there for the time is the* CAPITAL OF EUROPE, where the *most illustrious, noble, elegant,* and *tasteful* members of society assemble." Such an affected style alone might justify Jerrold's friend James Hannay's labeling the newspaper "The Fawning Post." To bring out Jenkins' intolerable hauteur, Jerrold quotes more of the preamble: "Every seat in every part of it was occupied, and if *those objectionable spectators were there* —those gentlemen of ambiguous gentility, the fashionable couriers, valets, *tailors,* and *shoemakers,* who obtain admission to the pit on the strength of knowing the measure of some actor or actress's foot—*they, and their frowsy dames,* were so nailed *to their benches* as not to offend the eye." [7] Jerrold footnotes this quotation and rightly so, for its arrogance and snobbishness sound more like Jerrold's own satiric creation than a serious preface to a review of an opera.

Jenkins is pictured as more concerned with the genteel society present than with the opera itself. The splendor with which he surrounds himself is made a recurrent contrast to the smallness of his own character: "Behold him in his glory in the opera pit—and then view him, as we a hundred times have seen him, creeping furtively from his three-pair back to buy his herring, or the green luxury of water cresses." [8] A later paper develops Jenkins' pretentious gentility by having him propose that nettles be eaten by shoemakers, tailors, and others of low society to purify their blood "to something like patrician sweetness." [9] In the next issue of *Punch* Jerrold prints two pieces of fictitious testimony telling how Peter Gooseton, a tailor, and Alexander Nobby, a shoemaker, changed after taking nettles. Gooseton writes that "the 'frowsiness' of which Mr. Jenkins spoke is utterly evaporated, given place to a delicious smell of something between lavender-water and musk; this, as I am told, being the real odour of high life." [10] The Shoemaker lost his "vulgar hump-back" and now feels as good as any earl.

When Jenkins makes one of his rare criticisms of the opera itself, Jerrold, quoting from the *Morning Post* review of *Athelwold,* satirizes a style so affected as to exclude any sense: "The chief defect of his drama is an utter want of *chronological allocation of its tone,* which could only have been afforded by *that costumed thought* which is so rarely acquired by the dramatist." Jerrold chides him and asks, "What do you mean, Jenkins? 'Costumed thought!' What is that? Thought in full-dress, of course. But Jenkins, pray write to be understood—don't affect 'too well'—condescend to be a man of the world—in a word, be a Man of the

People, Jenkins!" [11] "Man of the People" soon became Jenkins'
nickname both in cartoons and in future essays written by Jerrold,
Thackeray, and others.

Forster himself was most energetic in his calling and is said on
one occasion to have obtained admission, in the interest of *The
Morning Post,* to a Waterloo banquet at Apsley House, by disguis-
ing himself as one of the extra servants.[12] This incident may have
been the basis for Jerrold's hinting that Jenkins was once a foot-
man, but he explains that his satire is directed at the livery of his
soul:

> Not that his body, but that his soul is in livery, are we compelled to
> flog him with nettle-tops. Yes: his soul! Look, reader: peep in at the
> brain of Jenkins (you must use a glass, by the way, of great magnifying
> power). There, perched on *pia mater,* is what certain anatomists call
> the soul. With different men it takes different shapes. In the brain of
> Jenkins it is shaped like a Lilliput monkey, and there it sits, like the
> larger monkeys on the barrel-organs of those pedestrian virtuosi: (as
> Jenkins himself would say) who grind you off a hap-orths of Mozart or
> Donizetti. There is the monkey soul of Jenkins! And see you not his
> nether monkey, glowing in red plush? That is Jenkins' soul in full livery;
> and for that soul, so habited, we must (it is a public duty) continue to
> flog Jenkins.[13]

Jerrold not only deflates Jenkins and the opera with the sartorial-
anatomical analysis of his character, but conjures up in the sentence about the "nether monkey glowing in red plush" a coarse,
comical image of Jenkins as a baboon, an animal with a distinctive
rump of bare red calluses. Jerrold weaves the earlier attacks into
the present one by repeating Jenkins' bombastic words, such as
"virtuosi," and by alluding to his inane suggestion that the lower
classes eat nettles, which leads Jerrold to "flog him with nettle-
tops."

Thackeray's contributions to the Jenkins papers are more re-
strained than Jerrold's and are directed mostly at Jenkins' pretentious and uneducated use of French to raise the dignity of his
prose. Thackeray wrote "Punch's Parting Tribute to Jenkins":

> The illustrious nobody who has long afforded our readers much
> amusement, cannot be consigned to the obscurity from which we re-
> luctantly dragged him, without some appropriate memorial of his value
> and pretension. The annexed engraving, intended for that purpose, is a
> magnified design for a tobacco-stopper, to be cast—need we add—in

brass. The inscription in Jenkins-French has been submitted to the
Editor of the Morning Post, who perfectly reciprocates the sentiments
expressed in it.

> Oh!, Jenkins, homme du peuple—mangez bien,
> Désormais avec toi nous ferons rien,
> Vous êtes tout usé—chose qui montre la corde
> Nos lecteurs étaient mal de toi d'abord:
> Allez-vous-en—votre bâton coupez vite,
> En Ponch jamais votre nom—désormais sera dite.[14]

Jenkins turned out, however, not to be *"tout usé,"* and Thackeray's parting tribute proved to be premature. In the next volume
Thackeray helped to revive him in "Gems from Jenkins": "We are
inclined to think that Jenkins writes bad French, not because he
knows no better, but because in the fashionable world good
French would not be understood. They don't like it there. They
like their French loaded and doctored like their wine; and J.
———— knowing his public will only consume a bad article, sup-
plies that bad article to their hearts' content." [15] Actually, Forster
did not know French well. Henry Vizetelly, a contemporary journalist and publisher, relates an anecdote regarding a French
spoonerism made by Forster at a small party in Paris:

> While the dinner was being served one of the waiters persistently
> left the room door open, to the evident annoyance of Forster, who was
> sitting near to it. The latter knew only a few words of French, but
> fancied he knew sufficient for the occasion. So, waving his hand in
> rather an imperious manner, and unintentionally transposing a phrase
> he had often heard used, and thought he had it pat upon his tongue,
> he said to the offending waiter, "Garçon, portez la ferme! s'il vous
> plaît." The garçon, of course, stared amazed, and we diners, I am sorry
> to say, were all rude enough to roar with laughter.[16]

Soon Jenkins almost disappeared completely from the pages of
Punch, but the editorial office received so many letters inquiring
about his fate that Jerrold finally replied to his readers in such a
way as not to disappoint them completely: "Letters, 'thick as the
leaves of Vallombrosa,' come upon us, demanding the whereabouts of Jenkins? Some of the writers—we forgive the slander—
boldly aver that we, *Punch,* have killed, murdered outright, the
said Jenkins. We loved him too much; too deeply were we indebted to him to slay the flunky: no, the man was serviceable to

us." He then describes how he has looked high and low for him in the various haunts of London and has finally discovered him "mesmerised past hope of recovery at a neighbouring pot-house. We saw him and immediately put him on the paper. Yes, gentle reader, Jenkins, who has so oft delighted you, is in a trance. Should he, however, recover—should he by any accident return to pen and ink—depend upon it you shall have the earliest notion of his doings. In the meantime Jenkins, 'rosy dreams and slumbers soft.' Farewell, Jenkins." [17] This article, and not Thackeray's, proved to be the real farewell to Jenkins. By leaving him in a trance with slumbers light, Jerrold allows his readers to hope for Jenkins' reappearance in future issues of *Punch*. Two years later, in 1846, and again in 1848, Jerrold fulfills his promise by having Jenkins appear at a royal wedding and later at Drury Lane to comment upon *Monte Cristo;* but, for all intents and purposes, he was a *"chose qui montre la corde"* in 1844.

II   *Tales*

Considering that Jerrold wrote over a hundred pieces of short fiction, a surprisingly small number of them are devoted to social or political satire. Mostly he wrote tales designed to illustrate or to teach a moral lesson (which he often labelled "moralities") or farcical tales aimed simply to amuse. Although he published his stories in numerous magazines, such as the *Monthly Magazine, Bentley's Miscellany,* and the *Freemason's Quarterly Review,* most of them appeared in Theodore Hook's *New Monthly Magazine* which, because of its emphasis upon humorous and didactic "Original Papers," was ideally suited to Jerrold's temperament. A few years earlier Samuel Warren had complained to the editor of *Blackwood's Magazine* that Jerrold was marring the respectability of that distinguished periodical by his "vulgar" stories. Hook, on the other hand, published no less than thirty-six tales by Jerrold between 1837 and 1841, at which date he unhappily lost his Rabelaisian contributor to *Punch.*

In a Christmas supplement of the *Illustrated London News,* Jerrold wrote his most ambitious fairy story or morality, *The Sick Giant and the Doctor Dwarf.* Although nominally addressed to children, it contains imaginative suggestions and philosophic symbols that only adults could fully understand. It opens with the conventional "Once upon a time, there lived a Giant and a

Dwarf." [18] Whereas most of Jerrold's other tales have their settings in specific lands such as Singapore, Bassora, and Beauvais, this tale is set "far away, away across the sea" on an island—the universal unnamed never-never land soon to be populated by Edward Lear with Bong-trees, Jumblies, and Daddy Long Legs, and to which Victorians could turn in order to forget for a moment the confusion surrounding them caused by poverty, science, and technology.

The dwarfs who inhabit the island owe many of their characteristics to Jonathan Swift's Houyhnhnms of *Gulliver's Travels:* "truth and wisdom came to them as with the air they drew"; "a harmony of thought and action was their daily, household music"; and they lived "without grief or envy; and died, as flowers die, without a pang." They discover a giant on their beach who is suggestive of Gulliver, but Jerrold then changes Swift's story to suit his own purposes. As in *Gulliver's Travels,* there is a council that tries to decide the fate of Bakkuk, the giant. The majority of the citizens want him killed, but the wizard Zim, who had learned the beginning and progress of all natural things by having been nourished in the egg of an ostrich, suggests that they first inquire if he has any good in him.

Although the giant proceeds to roam the island and scream and drink wine until his face grows purple, Zim still opposes those who rule for his death and introduces the moral of the tale: "You shall see how this evil will become goodness. You shall learn that it is nobler to reform than to destroy." Zim discovers that the giant's revels are due to a disease and fever from which he is suffering, and he has the islanders slowly nurse him back to health. He then teaches him to till the land and harvest the crops, and "thus the labours of the Giant filled the island with blessings; and the Giant was blessed in the rewards of his labours—in the wages of respect and love he enjoyed of his masters." Zim's advice is realized: "Better to teach than to kill."

The tale could be read as simply a variation on the old story of the ferocious lion who became friendly upon having a thorn removed from his foot, but many of the explicit criticisms of English society that Jerrold was leveling years earlier in *Punch* are clearly implied in this tale. His crusade for the abolition of capital punishment is represented by Zim's argument to reform rather than to destroy. His attacks upon callous legislators like Alderman Laurie brought out that punishment is often inflicted because officials cannot understand the defendant's point of view; similarly, the islanders judge Bakkuk solely upon his riotous and drunken behavior. But it is only Zim who dares go beyond appearances to seek the cause of the problems and to bring about the islanders' sympathy and help instead of their condemnation of the giant. The conclusion suggests that education is not only more noble than destruction but will lead to the amelioration of the condition of all mankind. It will also be recalled that Jerrold, like Carlyle, denounced the "cash nexus" as the sole relationship between the worker and employer. Bakkuk's rewards, the respect and love of his master, are what Jerrold and Carlyle demanded of all employers if England was to prosper.

Jerrold, who was fond of devils, put them to good use in his plays, essays, and stories. In the play *The Devil's Ducat* (1830), a devil appears as the personification of Mammon to tempt Astolfo, who "dares be villain but dares not be poor." Jerrold also wrote an essay for the *New Monthly Magazine* entitled "Some Account of a Stage Devil" (1838), in which he reveals his wide knowledge of Mephistophelian lore. After surveying authorities and their writings on devils from Cornelius Agrippa to Olaus Magnus, he proceeds to analyze stage devils. He condemns the present "signpost devil," the cheapened caricature to which playgoers were accustomed, and praises the German actor Wieland for giving mystery back to the devil and making him a deeper, more forceful stage character.

A year after *The Devil's Ducat* appeared, Jerrold wrote a story with a similar theme called "The Tutor Fiend and his Three Pupils" which was published in the *Monthly Magazine*. This morality, full of the grotesque and melodramatic, is a variation of Chaucer's "Pardoner's Tale": it tells the story of a father who wanted his sons tutored in the art of "getting on." Rapax ("greed") entrances his pupils with a fascination for gold. They all go to an uncivilized island, bringing guns, disease, and superstition with them: "In fine, the island was civilized." [19] Rapax becomes the king, but upon his death the oppressed natives rush into his home to take his gold while two of the brothers flee, leaving one behind to be hanged because he cannot pay his brothers for his passage. Then one of the two remaining brothers kills the other for his treasure but unknowingly buries the keys to the treasure chest with the body. He goes mad and beats himself to death against the chest.

Rapax is a fiend that personifies the commercial spirit of England in the early 1830's; both the settlement in Australia and the commercialism in India are suggested by Jerrold's satirical account of civilizing the island by the tutor and his pupils. Fifteen years later Harriet Martineau's *Dawn Island* balances Jerrold's account by singing the virtues and joys that the English merchants bring to an ignorant, savage group of islanders.

Another devil appears in the "Wine Cellar" (1837), a tale that curiously anticipates Edgar A. Poe's "The Cask of Amontillado" (1846).[20] One night Stephen Curlew, a frugal goldsmith in the reign of Charles II, is visited in his home by a cloaked stranger who asks him to cut a seal in a ring to depict Bacchus squeezing grape juice into the cup of death. One suspects the mysterious stranger to be satanic when he is described as having a brick-red face and coal-black moustache; and, during his ironic conversation with Stephen about the ring, his purpose becomes clear as they speak of death, by which Stephen means the design in the ring and the stranger means Stephen's destruction. The stranger bewilders Stephen with such ironic innuendoes as "thou art yet but a poor apprentice at Death."

When the stranger returns later for his ring, he tempts Stephen to take his first drink of wine and leaves him craving the liquor. Alone with one remaining flask, Stephen's newly acquired vice leads him to take it to the cellar in order to hide it from his workmen. While nailing it in a secret crypt, he discovers that, in his stupor, he has driven the nails from the wrong side and has sealed himself in. Jerrold adds a few vivid details to the macabre conclusion by describing the scene (while declaring the description unnecessary): "Shall we describe how he clawed and struck at the door, now in the hope to wrench a nail, and now to alarm the breathing men above? No; we will not swell upon the horror. . . ." One hundred and seventy-five years later his skeleton is discovered by some laborers and near it stands the wine flask.

At this point, Jerrold tacks on a paragraph of comic moralizing that weirdly contrasts with the earlier forbidding and horrifying tone:

"Oh, ye heads of families! and oh, ye thrifty, middle-aged bachelors, boarding with families, or growing mouldy by yourselves, never, while ye live, forget the terrible end of Stephen Curlew. And oh, ye heads of families—and oh, ye aforesaid bachelors, albeit ye have only one bottle left, never, *never* nail up the wine cellar!" [21]

This burlesque of moral endings is in keeping with the cult of the comic-horrible, which is best exemplified in R. H. Barham's *The Ingoldsby Legends or Mirths and Marvels* (1840) and today by "black humor." Jerrold published "The Wine Cellar" in 1837, the same year that Barham's grotesque tales began to appear in *Bentley's Miscellany*.

Jerrold's burlesque of moral endings finds numerous counterparts in *The Ingoldsby Legends*. "A Lay of St. Gengulphus" tells the story of St. Gengulphus who, after his return from the Holy Land, was murdered and dismembered by his wife and her paramour. Although Gengulphus is miraculously made whole again by the end of the tale, Barham is more concerned with rendering the gruesome murder with comic effect than he is in imparting the lesson of heroic virtue contained in the *Acta Sanctorum*:

Thus limb from limb, they dismember'd him
So entirely, that e'en when they came to his wrists,
With those great sugar-nippers they nipp'd off his "flippers,"
As the Clerk, very flippantly, term'd his fists.

Barham adds to the tale a three-stanza comic moral in which he warns married pilgrims not to wander away from home and clerks to stay close to their books; then he addresses the ladies:

Above all, you gay ladies, who fancy neglect
In your spouses, allow not your patience to fail
But remember Gengulphus's wife!—and reflect
On the moral enforced by our terrible tale! [22]

Jerrold's warning to heads of families and bachelors to remember "the terrible end of Stephen Curlew" is in the same comic spirit, therefore, as Barham's moral. The major difference between "A Wine Cellar" and *The Ingoldsby Legends* lies in the tales themselves. In Barham's stories and verses, the continuous mingling of the comic with the grotesque is carried over into the moral. Jerrold's tale, however, is entirely serious; and the comic moral comes as a weird surprise.

Two years later, in "The Mayor of Hole-Cum-Corner," [23] Jerrold
uses the theme of the Faustian pact. Mayor Tobias Aconite (a
typical Jerroldian name meaning "wolfsbane") has unjustly sen-
tenced a man to be flogged for stealing a gander. When it is discovered that the gander was only lost, the whole town turns
against Tobias. At this point, he is visited, like Curlew, by a mysterious stranger, only the supernatural aspect of his person is more
quickly disclosed as he sits with one leg in Tobias' fireplace while
he is talking until it glows bright red. He offers to sell the mayor a
cloak that will make him appear virtuous and enable him to win
back the confidence of his townspeople. In return for the cloak,
Tobias must give his soul; but he rejects the offer, declaring that
he wants a good conscience, not a false appearance. Then the
devil extracts Tobias's soul and leads his body, instilled with an
evil nature, to roam the streets, get drunk, and beat his wife while
the "true" Tobias helplessly watches his image disgrace him.
When the devil then tempts him again with the cloak, it is still
refused. Tobias becomes himself again, and ironically his wife
begins treating him charitably for the first time in his life. Meanwhile, a royal Spaniard has arrived in England to marry, and Tobias rallies the town to greet him; but his evil counterpart reappears, insults the Spaniard, and is ordered beheaded. He vanishes,
and good Tobias, now faced with death, is again tempted by the
devil; but he still refuses the cloak. Just as the ax falls, Tobias has
his place again filled by his evil counterpart. The lesson of heroic
virtue that triumphs over hypocrisy and slander is cast as a moral
allegory that clumsily anticipates R. L. Stevenson's *The Strange
Case of Dr. Jekyll and Mr. Hyde* (1886). It is only after Tobias
comes to terms with his evil nature that he can take intelligent
control over his future and win the good will of the townspeople.

The last story to make use of the devil is "Ephraim Rue: the
'Victim of Society'" (1841). Ephraim, who believes that he is
"made for society," unhappily seems condemned to live alone. One
night, after he complains, "What's the world without a party?," [24] a
stranger in regal dress comes to his door and invites him to a ball
at Haunch Lodge, promising him he will dance with the squire's
wife. As in the preceding story, a covenant is drawn up, in which
the devil grants Ephraim a life in society with the stipulation that
he must endure the devil's company whenever he is alone. The
stranger is easily identified by his grim-looking footmen and the

coach's ability to fly; but, to leave no doubt, he gives Ephraim his card on which the name Beelzebub appears.

After the pleasures of the ball, Ephraim plans how he can beat the devil at his game; and he has Nick, the parish boy, come to live with him. Because of his sudden usefulness, Nick grows proud and insolent; and Ephraim plans to marry in order to be able to dismiss the impudent boy. When he marries a wealthy woman, he is now not only in society but of it. When his wife grows ill and when he is forced to go out for medicine, he meets the devil. Just then a woman passes by and Ephraim offers her money if she will give him hospitality, which she does; but, when her husband appears, he misunderstands the situation and knocks Ephraim down. He is now disgraced in the public's eyes, and his wife wants a separation. He plans bigamy, becomes a drunkard, a rake, and a gambler. One day he joins a company of three men who turn out to be burglars. When Ephraim is told to climb into a window, he is shot to death by an earlier acquaintance.

It is interesting that both Tobias and Ephraim are tempted with nothing so grand as knowledge or power but with the benefits of hypocrisy and genteel society. In both instances, the Victorian devils are keenly aware of social values in the early 1840's and they offer fantasies that reflect the actual temptations and aspirations of the Victorian middle class.

"Mr. Peppercorn at Home" is interesting because it anticipates by five years the theme of Dickens' *A Christmas Carol*. Mr. Peppercorn, an unfeeling miser, is converted to benevolence upon seeing a ghost which inspires him with terror and pity. The theme is worked out, however, in details totally unlike Dickens' book. Peppercorn is called from his stark Lincolnshire estate to London because his tenements there have long been unrented as a result of tales of murder and ghosts. It is noteworthy that Jerrold, who usually sacrifices atmospheric descriptions in favor of action and dialogue, uses descriptive details to suggest character and mood. The Lincolnshire estate and its surroundings, for example, objectify Peppercorn's cold, unfeeling, severe character. The reader is told that in "the last frost a cat had been found frozen to death at the fireside." The house is old, dilapidated, and stark as its owner: "The Hall was a huge, shapeless pile, pierced with here and there a window—indeed, it was a whitewashed barn, with casements. Time and tempest had done their work, and the very penetralia of the building were now open to sun and rain." Even his dog and horse reflect his parsimonious character: the horse is half-starved with a tail as "bare as a carrot"; the dog, too weak to bark, can only wheeze at its master.

Arrived in London, Peppercorn disregards the stories surrounding his tenements; and, to save the price of a hotel, he goes to spend the night there. Jerrold creates the mood of terror by describing the tenements with atmospheric details borrowed from the Gothic novels: "They formed a long, dismal line of blackened brick. Each house, viewed by itself, with its uncurtained, cheerless windows, looked grim and desolate—an eyeless skull. Spiders wove their webs in the doorway, and the sparrows chirped from the smokeless chimney. There seemed the curse of crime or law on the buildings: surely, some murder had been done there. . . ." [25] Peppercorn is subjected to a few eerie experiences, such as seeing the ghost of his dead sister, from whom he had extorted the tenements; but, as in the novels of Clara Reeve and Ann Radcliffe, the supernatural suffers a rational explanation: the ghosts turn out to be a band of vagabonds and scoundrels who have spread the tales of horror to keep tenants away in order that they might continue to live there rent free. Nevertheless, the imagined vision of his injured sister suffices to transform Peppercorn into a charitable man who repents his past miserliness, asks his mistreated nephew's forgiveness, and bestows his fortune upon him.

Jerrold wrote numerous miscellaneous moralities that set out to teach such lessons as charity, humbleness, thankfulness, sensibleness, generosity, and keeping busy. His usual method is to present a character who suffers some painful consequences for lacking one or more of these qualities, but he varies his specific techniques in each story. In "The Lesson of Life," for example, Jerrold uses a dream as the instrument of instruction. After a selfish old lord dismisses his woodsman, Rupert, for killing one of his favorite dogs that otherwise would have killed Rupert's son, the Lord is pictured as writhing in his sleep; and he has a long, involved dream in which Rupert reappears and his impoverished condition tempts him into intrigues, thefts, and murder plots; and, when he is about to be beheaded, the old Lord awakens "an altered man" and learns "to deal mercifully with our fellow-men, and thereby, in their day of destitution, to preserve them from the temptations of evil. . . ." [26]

This story, published four years before *A Christmas Carol*, bears, like "Mr. Peppercorn at Home," an interesting resemblance to it. Scrooge's dream, in which he is visited by the ghost of Jacob Marley and the three spirits of Christmas, causes him to repent his miserly habits and to become charitable. In both cases, an unfeeling, selfish old man, after being visited in a dream by the character from his past, is changed into a benevolent person.

One farcical story should be considered in conjunction with an observation made by Allardyce Nicoll about Jerrold's experimentation with dramatic technique. Nicoll singles out Jerrold from his contemporaries for his experimental use of time sequences and the aside, and he suggests his modernity: "The 'aside,' of course, is a device of hoary antiquity, and in the drama of this period it is of constant occurrence. A reading of Jerrold's plays, however, will convince us that in his works these asides appear much more frequently than in the plays of his companions. At first sight, we are inclined to believe that they represent merely the abuse of what was a common failing, but a further examination suggests that they possess a deliberate purpose and that here Douglas Jerrold was holding forth his hand, if but weakly, to the author of *Strange Interlude*." [27]

Jerrold employs a similar technique in his farcical story "The Preacher Parrot." He uses a parrot that has the disturbing habit of announcing the truth at critical moments as a device by which people's true thoughts are revealed. The technical difference between this device and the aside is that others in the story can hear the parrot; on the other hand, it is like the aside in purpose since it is the vehicle by which one discovers a character's private thoughts. The parrot passes through four people's hands, and its outspokenness affects the lives of all four. The parrot's third owner, for instance, gives a select party ostensibly to celebrate the birthday of Belinda, her only unmarried daughter, but actually to find her a husband. The mother addresses a banker's son: "'All married, except my dear Belinda; and it would break my heart, I believe, to part with her. Yes, Sir,' said the mother, affected even by the probability of a separation, 'Belinda, sir, is—is' —. '*The last lot, gentlemen,—the last lot!*' cried the parrot." [28]

In one of his few satirical stories, Jerrold's "The Papers of a 'Gentleman-at-Arms'" surveys a number of contemporary fashions and events. The story of Gustavus Nibs' rise in London society as a gentleman-at-arms is told through a series of letters between Gustavus and his family and friends at home in Mousehole, Cornwall. The name "Nibs," a variant of the slang term "Nob," indicates Gus's sense of self-importance and social rank. After visiting the playhouses, he records his horror at the mob at Covent Garden where he went to see *Coriolanus:* "the pack of vagabonds" were "bellowing, threatening, stamping at the noble Roman." Gus obviously identifies himself through his newly acquired nobility with Coriolanus and his scorn for the plebeians. He also writes of the local gossip about Covent Garden, which was attempting to hire the tragedian, William Macready.

Jerrold ridicules the vogue of painting women according to certain flower types, such as in "Daisies of Delicacy," and the extreme sentimentalism which they foster: "Every 'Pink of Loveliness,' yea, every 'Dahlia of the Dowagers,' seems made of sugar, and ready to melt in the mouth. The old school is all wiriness and severity—the new, sugar and spice, and everything nice." Portraits of literary heroines were also popular, and Jerrold remarks on the absurdity of trying to render a fictitious character in realistic detail: "With the assistance of modern art, you may know the precise length of Pamela's nose, and swear to the lips of Lady Montague's Roxalana."

Using Gus as a mouthpiece again, Jerrold reviews various paintings that were on exhibition in 1838 and reflects the typical public reaction to Joseph Turner's works. Ruskin's first volume of *Modern Painters,* in which he defends Turner's "truth" and explains his distortion of topography, was still six years away; and, despite Turner's fame and wealth, the general public found his work bewildering and unsatisfying. Jerrold disparages his "Phryne Going to the Public Bath as Venus," and he ridicules "Modern Italy—the Pifferari": "At first we took the picture for a framed and uncleaned palette. . . ." [29] He singles out for his highest praise the more conventional "Merry Christmas in the Baron's Hall" by Daniel Maclise, the historical painter. Maclise's paintings, in contrast to Turner's, were very elaborate compositions that emphasized clear and definite form; therefore, precision and completeness of outline were preserved at all costs.

Gus is a combination of a ridiculous fool, who strives to advance in the social scale, and a sensible spokesman for Jerrold's views on art, drama, books, fashions, and current events. In the role of critic, he resembles Thackeray's "Michael Angelo Titmarsh," who, by the mid 1840's, was practically Thackeray's alter ego. Commissioned to review the annual exhibitions of paintings at the National Gallery and elsewhere, Thackeray contributed "Strictures on Pictures" to *Fraser's Magazine* for June, 1838, under the name "Michael Angelo Titmarsh." Jerrold was the first, however, to employ the device of a fictitious letter to embody his criticism: "Papers of a 'Gentleman-at-Arms' " began in March, 1838, and included discussions of players, books, fashions, and recreations of Londoners; in May, Jerrold began using Gus to review paintings. Thackeray may have borrowed the idea from Jerrold's series because, in the following month, he employed the same technique to review works of art in his first "Titmarsh" paper. Most of Thackeray's articles were restricted to the subject of paintings, but he occasionally used Titmarsh to expound upon other topics, such as his comic account of a dinner at a Paris Club, interspersed with gossip about Parisians, in "Memorials of Gormandising" (1841).[30]

The Coronation of Queen Victoria in 1837 was to be Gus's crowning achievement as a gentleman-at-arms. Jerrold ridicules the distortion of values men undergo to obtain social ranks by having Gus practice placing beef-pies on a table, as part of his corps' assignment to put various dishes before the Queen on the day of her coronation. Gus believes that "men have gained knighthood from meaner things than beef-steak pies." In a letter to his sister, Gus describes what he imagines the coronation will be like and promises to write her later to compare the actual ceremony with his imaginative version of it. That letter turns out to be a defense of his corps and his own recently acquired gentility against the "malice of a disappointed candidate for our purchasable laurels," who supposedly wrote in a newspaper or journal that the Gentleman-at-Arms marred the ceremony with "noisy gabble."

The pseudonymous editor of Gus's letters, Henry Brownrigg, notes that Gus offers no proof of the author of the slander; and the *Times*, which carried a detailed account of every phase of the Coronation, makes no mention of unruly behavior among the Gentlemen-at-Arms. Whether there actually was such a charge made in print or whether Jerrold contrived the situation is not certain, but Gus's defensive response is meant to poke fun at the oversensitive pride and to reveal the insecurity of those persons whose dignity is purchasable. At the end of the letter, however, Gus admits that "there *was* a little scrambling in the Abbey: perhaps a little whispering among us . . . for who at such a time and in such a place, could be all tranquillity?" [31] Despite all the practice of placing beef-pies before an imaginary queen, when Gus was in the midst of the actual ceremony, his awkwardness defeated his assumed dignity, suggesting that he might never acquire the refinement and composure that comes naturally to those born in the upper classes, and that his provincial character will continue to make his attempts to rise above his fellows in Mousehole appear ludicrous.

III *Novels*

Jerrold's three attempts at long sustained fiction were aimed at underscoring the political and social unrest of his times. Like Dickens and Thackeray, he branched out from journalism, sketches, and short fiction to novels; but, as it soon became clear that this genre was unsuited to him, journalism and drama remained his principal means of support. Nevertheless, *The Story of a Feather* (1843), *St. Giles and St. James* (1845–47), and *A Man Made of Money* (1848) were read and greatly admired by thousands of people, including Dickens, whose unqualified praise of these works may strike one today as odd.

The Story of a Feather originally appeared in serial form in *Punch* throughout the greater part of the two volumes of 1843. It was the only work of fiction that continued to maintain a popularity in any way comparable with that of the *Curtain Lectures*, after which it was the most frequently reprinted of Jerrold's works. It was the greatest success *Punch* had experienced up to that time, with the exception of the first *Almanac*. When the story was published as a book, Dickens wrote Jerrold that he "put the 'Story of a Feather' on a shelf (not an obscure one) where some other feathers are, which it shall help to show mankind which way the wind blows, long after *we* know where the wind comes from. I am quite delighted to find that you have touched the latter part again, and touched it with such a delicate and tender hand. It is a wise and beautiful book. I am sure I may venture to say so to you, for nobody consulted it more regularly and earnestly than I did, as it came out in *Punch*." [32]

Jerrold reverts to the technique employed by Charles Johnstone in his satire, *Chrysal, or The Adventures of a Guinea* (1760–65), which is narrated by a coin that passes through various social groups from Peru to London and that comments upon the dishonest motives of the various characters who appear along its journey. *The Story of a Feather* is narrated by an ostrich feather[33] from Africa that arrives in London, where it remains for most of the story to be passed through no less than twenty hands, from the poor to the rich, the innocent and the criminal, as it analyzes the characters of its various owners with its chief focus upon Patty Butler, a poor featherdresser, who is cruelly mistreated by society. The novel has a loose, episodic structure and a large cast of characters, many of whom are believable and whose reappearance throughout the story affords a semblance of unity, however contrived, to the episodes. The wide scope of the London setting includes pawnships, St. James's Palace, Drury Lane, a trial court, Newgate Prison, impoverished garrets, the home of a countess, and various London taverns. The reader almost forgets the device of the feather after Jerrold begins to focus upon his heroine, Patty Butler, in the fourth chapter, for it is her story that is being told.

By following the life of a central character, to whom all the other characters are in one way or another related, Jerrold gives the book a degree of unity that is lacking in *Chrysal*. On the other hand, it raises a technical problem that Johnstone and others did not have to face: the guinea, for instance, was free to move from place to place and comment discursively upon its travels and the people it met; but Jerrold's feather must never wholly lose sight of Patty Butler when it is in the possession of other characters not immediately related to her. When the feather is in the hands of Patty's landlady, Mrs. Crump, Patty is suddenly taken to Newgate on a mistaken charge of theft. She is then out of sight for six chapters until Jerrold arranges for Mrs. Crump to drop the feather accidentally and for Mike Trapley, the Newgate turnkey, to happen upon it and bring it to the prison, where it can continue its narrative of Patty's fate. It is only at this point that Jerrold is able to supply the reader with the events that led up to her arrest, which he accomplishes by having Patty's old protector, the apothecary Lintley, come to the prison to help her find justice: " 'Yet, tell me,' said the apothecary, 'for I must trace you step by step— tell me, what could have brought you here?' " Since Jerrold's point of view is necessarily limited to the location of the feather, this problem often arises. Whenever possible, he solves it by parentheses in which the feather begins "As I afterwards discovered" and then provides some necessary background information it could not have acquired first hand in its travels.

Sometimes Jerrold varies this technique to indulge in pure fantasy, as when he describes Mme. Spanneu's character by having her clothes gossip to the feather. When the feather is later carried to Drury Lane, the intimate details of the various actors of the time are supplied by a bodice "commonly worn . . . by the meaner people of the playhouse," which speaks for more than a chapter until the feather "learned all the past and present politics of the playhouse." [34]

Jerrold must also create incredible coincidences to place the feather in Patty's possession at critical moments. It has already been seen how Trapley happened upon the feather and carried it to Newgate. After the prison episode, the feather is taken to Drury Lane, and only after following a most circuitous route, in the course of which it changes hands nine times, does it return to Patty (by way of a traveling showman whose monkey drops the feather from its cap) in order to conclude the story by relating her happy marriage to a curate, a marriage that promises a reward of peace for her early trials in life.

Despite Blanchard Jerrold, who praises the story for "the natural way in which the feather travels," [35] the structure is obviously poorly conceived and worked out. This may be a result of the excessive freedom to distort reality that Jerrold had enjoyed for years in his farces, in which funny characters and absurd events took precedence over the illusion of reality and a unified plot. The popularity of this story lay in its appeal to pathos because of the character of Patty Butler, in its array of colorful characters, in its vivid descriptions of London squalor, and in its implicit and explicit moral indictments of society. Jerrold was at his height as a journalist in *Punch* while he was writing the weekly installments of the story, and such social issues as the injustice of the law courts, the irresponsibility of the upper classes, and the condition of the poor were readily carried over into fiction as his central themes.

Still, the popularity of the work cannot be attributed merely to its treatment of current social problems. The single most powerful appeal of the story arises from the theme of the social outcast, embodied in Patty Butler. With great emotional force Jerrold conveys the loneliness felt by a girl who is driven aimlessly through the poor parts of London. She first appears when her mother, her solitary protector in the world, is dying in a gloomy garret "in a long, dark lane on the north side of the Strand; in one of those noisome, pestilent retreats abutting on, yet hidden by, the wealth and splendour of the metropolis . . ." (116). Upon her mother's death, Patty is left totally alone to "venture in the roaring street." She is separated from the world by her virtue: "Unseen, unknown, are the divinities that—descending from garrets—tread the loud, foul, sordid, crowding highways of London. Spiritual presences, suffering all things, and in the injustice—most hard to turn to right—of our social purpose, living and smiling, daily martyrs to their creed of good" (122).

Her world swiftly becomes as absurd to her as Alice's Wonderland, for she is arrested for theft on charges made by a man who tried to molest her. Even though Naplightly, the constable, is eventually satisfied that she did not steal the man's watch, he forces her to ask his pardon "for having accosted him in the street" (127), thus humiliating her further. She is kept from utter destitution by the benevolent apothecary Lintley, who takes her into his home; but this kind gesture in the midst of a hostile world is quickly corrupted in the mind of Lintley's wife, who grows jealous of Patty and drives her back into isolation. Once again, she is arrested unjustly and imprisoned in Newgate. In the commotion of being arrested, all she can think of is Lintley, the only person whom she understands in a swirling angry world that makes no sense: "The recollection was again too much for her. She looked about her—at the faces hurrying around her, and smitten by the remembrance of her past sufferings—by her belief in future misery—she hid her face in her hands, and wept bitterly" (201).

In prison, Patty's existence gradually takes on the qualities of a gruesome nightmare. Mrs. Trapley, in a good-natured attempt to chastize Patty for not caring that others think her guilty, terrorizes her with a vivid description of the trip of condemned prisoners to Tyburn:

You don't know what it is, child, or you wouldn't talk in that way. Ha! my dear, it's very different to going with a party, and sitting at a window to see the poor things in the cart; that's very different to being one of 'em, you know. Innocence, my dear, is all very well; but I don't know any innocence that could bear to be stared at by thousands of people, all looking as if they had red-hot eyes upon you. And then to see the whole street swimming about you—and to have the blood like boiling lead in your ears—for a dear soul as was reprieved told me all about it—and how all the men and women looked like stony-faced devils round him—and how he heard some of 'em laugh, it went like a knife into his heart—and how as the cart rumbled along, he prayed for stones to open and bury him—and how when he got to Tyburn, ha! my dear, he was proved as innocent as you are, and yet he felt all this —and who, as I was saying, when he got to Tyburn—but you don't listen to me? (234)

The nightmarish effect is strongly reinforced through the demoni-acal Mrs. Gaptooth, who pursues Patty like a hunted animal and drives her into hiding. Patty tells Lintley how she was persecuted: "Day after day she came to the house—I never went abroad but she followed me. I know not how it was, I felt for her a loathing I never knew for any human creature. I could not endure her. And then I heard strange stories of her; and so that I might free myself of her, unknown to anybody, I hid here" (205). Mrs. Gaptooth, who persists like an evil dream from which Patty cannot wake, follows her even into Newgate, where she is helpless and, no longer able to run, is made to withstand her relentless terror:

As she approached, the face of the girl changed to marble paleness; her eyes looked darker and darker; and her mouth became rigidly curved, with an expression of mingled fear and scorn. Once, as from some ungovernable impulse, she shivered from head to sole. She grasped the arms of the chair, and still shrank back as the old woman came nearer to her. She seemed possessed by some terrible antipathy— some irrepressible loathing—that, in its intensity, made her powerless. Still Mrs. Gaptooth, with her undaunted smiles, advanced. She was about to lay her hand upon Patty, when, with almost a shriek, the girl leaped from her chair. (237)

It is easy to see why Dickens praised this work: it reflects his own point of view and contains themes and characters that had al-ready distinguished his novels and were to continue in his future books. Like Little Nell or Oliver Twist, Patty Butler, the central character, is a child of incorruptible virtue; just as Oliver with-stood the evil power of the Artful Dodger and Fagin, so Patty could not be forced into prostitution by the grim Mrs. Gaptooth.

Patty's stay in Newgate provides a horrifying picture of that place that compares well with Pickwick's travail in the Fleet. The benevolent apothecary Lintley, who takes Patty into his home, is another Mr. Brownlow. The Reverend Mr. Inglewood, who exposes and triumphs over hypocrisy and immorality and who finally marries Patty, is the saintly embodiment of virtues which Dickens extols in his own good characters.

Jerrold's longest work of fiction, *St. Giles and St. James,* appeared in monthly installments between 1845 and 1847 in his own *Shilling Magazine.* The work traces from birth the lives of two Londoners, St. Giles and St. James, and shows how paradoxically close together their lives are bound. St. Giles derives his name from St. Giles's in the Fields, a poor parish in the most westerly part of Holborn, in which St. Giles's Rookery and other wretched tenements were located. St. James is named after the exclusive area of London that includes the Tudor palace and St. James's Park. The contrast resembles the one employed by Disraeli in *Sybil, or the Two Nations,* except that Jerrold's St. James is not only wealthy but an aristocrat.

Jerrold sets forth his purpose of social reform in the Preface to the 1851 volume:

It has been my endeavour to show in the person of St. Giles the victim of an ignorant disregard of the social claims of the poor upon the rich; of the governed million upon the governing few; to present— I am well aware how imperfectly; but with no wilful exaggeration of the portraiture—the picture of the infant pauper reared in brutish ignorance; a human waif of dirt and darkness. Since the original appearance of this story, the reality of this picture, in all its vital and appalling horror, has forced itself upon the legislature; has engaged its anxious humanising sympathies.[36]

Like *The Story of a Feather,* the plot of *St. Giles and St. James* revolves around an outcast of society who "was a hunted, persecuted wretch; life to him was a miserable disease; a leprosy of soul that made him alone in a breathing world" (115). But, unlike Patty Butler, Oliver Twist, and Little Nell, St. Giles is a fallible child character who actually commits crimes. Taken from his mother, who was found half dead on a wintry London night, he is reared by the Aniseed family. He grows up with the moral code of poor street urchins, and at seven he steals St. James's hat. Tom

Blast, an Artful Dodger, becomes his "Newgate father," and tempts him into stealing St. James's horse; for which crime St. Giles, at fifteen years of age, is transported for life to Botany Bay. After a period of nine years, his love of England drives him back to London, where he looks for his mother and discovers that she has died during his absence and that he now has a half-brother named Jingo, who is Blast's latest protégé in crime. St. Giles then gets involved in the parliamentary elections at Liquorish, working for the Blues, who support St. James, against the Yellows who finally win with their candidate, the misanthropic muffin-maker Capstick, who was St. Giles's wise counselor years ago and who now lives with Bright Jem Aniseed.

Capstick was supported by Ebenezer Snipeton, a usurer, who saw St. James as a rival for the affection of his wife, Clarissa. Snipeton hides her away from society; but Crossbones, a physician who seeks court preferment, kidnaps her, thereby hoping to please St. James whose sympathy for the mistreated Clarissa leads him to free her as Snipeton, informed of her whereabouts by Blast, attacks St. James and is killed. St. Giles, Blast, and St. James are all arrested. Blast confesses his crimes and dies in prison; St. James is acquitted; and St. Giles is condemned to be hanged, only to be pardoned later through the combined efforts of St. James and Capstick.

The plot, full of improbable events, is contrived mainly to illustrate the corrupting influence of society upon the youth of the London poor. The characters are subordinate to the theme of social protest, and their actions are too obviously guided by the unseen puppeteer. Jerrold typically bends the action to fit his social theme when he makes St. Giles's life coincide with St. James's at crucial points in order to compare the two social orders. St. James, for instance, is born six months after St. Giles, "his youthful brother—for in this story St. Giles and St. James must fraternise . . ." (17). St. Giles's two thefts and subsequent pardons bring them together and illustrate both St. Giles's predestined life of crime and St. James's charitable attitude toward the poor. The elections and Snipeton's death again join the two and purport to show that

St. James had been schooled even by St. Giles: taught the best and highest lesson of life from his association with the born outcast and baby felon. The man of conventional nobility had learned to see through want, and misery, and crime, the natural man: still the born aristocrat of all created things, however degraded from the hour of his birth by the ignorance and injustice of our social conditions (391–92).

Jerrold clumsily anticipates Hardy's naturalism by having the actions of his characters largely determined by an apparently haphazard series of antecedent circumstances; but, whereas Hardy's characters are often depicted as the helpless victims of cosmic powers, Jerrold's are viewed as victims of a cruelly impersonal society. This outlook frequently forced both authors to contrive implausible plots and to sacrifice a presentation or an analysis of their character's internal conflicts.

The actions and motives of St. Giles and St. James, however, do not convincingly support the two main themes that society is totally responsible for the corruption of poor youths and that St. James learned to see the natural man beneath the tatters of poverty. One of Jerrold's contemporaries, perceiving that there are "conclusions that do not naturally follow the premises, and effects traced to causes that have not produced them," [37] felt dissatisfied with this novel.

One of the reasons for this failing was Jerrold's revision of the work for the collected edition. He revised the story in an attempt to be more just to the aristocrat: "I will only add that upon and after revision of this story, I cannot think myself open to the charge of bedizening St. Giles at the cost of St. James; or of making Hog Lane the treasury of all the virtues to the moral sacking of May Fair" (iii-iv). In the original version, it is simply stated that, at the end of the trial, St. James "went abroad, made the grand tour, returned, married a duke's daughter, and to the end of his days, supported to the utmost the dignity of his order." [38] In the revision, Jerrold has added over half a page in order to explain St. James's discovery of respect for himself and for St. Giles, and his subsequent pilgrimages to the Hog Lanes to make "noble amends in his maturer years for the harmful vanities of his earlier life" (392).

Unfortunately, no evidence exists in the story to indicate that St. James has undergone any such change to make for a reconciliation between the worlds of May Fair and Hog Lane. He is never even portrayed as indulging any "harmful vanities"; on the contrary, he is pictured as a sympathetic character who twice before withdrew criminal charges against St. Giles. Jerrold was constantly defending himself against charges of bitterness and acridity towards the rich; and in his revision, by suddenly suppressing his natural bias in a belated attempt to ennoble St. James, he falsifies the original St. James, whose wealth and position served mainly as a foil to St. Giles's wretchedness.

The other theme, society's disservice to the poor, is not convincingly dramatized in either version. Like Theodore Dreiser in *Sister Carrie*, Jerrold relies upon strong emotional appeal and upon improbable events to accuse society of destroying his innocent protagonist and to excuse him of every criminal act. Although St. Giles "would steal with all his heart and all his soul" (60), Jerrold completely exonerates him of any responsibility because "he was born and bred to steal; he came into the world to do it, and he would notably fulfil his mission. Such was the strengthened belief of young St. Giles, when, at fourteen, and for the second time, he came back to the world across the threshold of Bridewell. Such was his creed: the only creed his world has taught him" (60). Here again we see Jerrold's naturalism, one suggestive of Zola and Hardy in his emphasis upon environment and heredity as the factors which determine an individual's fate: St. Giles "was born and bred to steal."

St. Giles's world is composed of fellow prisoners and the tempter Tom Blast; it is "the world of Hog Lane," where "the foot-pad, the pickpocket, the burglar, had been his teachers: they had sent him copies, and he had written them in his brain for life-long wisdom" (39). In order to justify the theme of the corruption of youth, Jerrold omits any mention of the kindly and moral Aniseed family, who reared St. Giles; and he never adequately explains how he moved from the Aniseeds' influence to that of Tom Blast. Once the world of Hog Lane is conceded, however, Jerrold makes a strong case to prove that St. Giles, despite his crimes, is as innocent as Patty Butler. From that point on, the two worlds of St. Giles and St. James are developed as realistic, isolated entities like Disraeli's two nations: it is only when Jerrold forces communication between them in his revision of the story that both are artistically weakened.

St. Giles and St. James derives its appeal from its diversity of characters who can be visualized as clearly as if they walked the stage and from its emotional scenes that touch upon social conditions in which Jerrold's readers were exceedingly interested. The story originally appeared in a magazine designed specifically for the poorer classes, who would naturally take pleasure in the adventures of the outcast St. Giles and who would see their own problems worked out each month in the *Shilling Magazine* during the hungry 1840's.

A Man of Money, the third and last of Jerrold's long pieces of fiction, was published in monthly parts of four chapters each over a period of six months during 1848. Dickens had been producing his novels in parts for twelve years; most parts of Thackeray's first novel, *Vanity Fair*, had appeared; and the proposal was made to Jerrold to follow suit. Free now of his *Weekly Newspaper* and *Shilling Magazine*, and having no serial work in *Punch*, he set to work on the story. The venture was successful, but not nearly to the same degree as the novels of Dickens and Thackeray. For the third time, despite his treating the same themes as Dickens did, his novel failed to achieve wide acceptance. The basic recurrent feature is his didacticism, but *A Man Made of Money* employs some radical changes in technique that sets it apart from his first two stories.

When the first part of *A Man Made of Money* was published, a reviewer for the *Athenaeum* complained that the story's hero was unbelievable and that among all the characters "there is nothing of much greater value than a paper heart (*without* the currency stamp)." [39] Since the critic had read only one sixth of the work, he admits that his judgment may be premature. Six years later, when the story was reprinted in volume form, a reviewer for the same magazine, recognizing Jerrold's deliberate use of fantasy, praised the book, comparing it to some of the great European novelists: "The 'Man Made of Money' reminds us at once of Hoffmann, Chamisso, and Balzac. Of the first, in the mingling of the grotesque and the terrible; of Chamisso in the simplicity and air of truthfulness in the characters who are outside the circle of terror, and of Balzac, because Jericho's skin is a more genuine 'Peau de Chagrin' than that which forms the basis of the story so named, by the French writer." [40] James Hannay, who discussed the work at length in the *Atlantic Monthly Magazine*, concluded: "In short, I esteem this Jerrold's best book,—the one which contains most of his mind." [41]

Sabilla, the wife of Solomon Jericho, nags her husband for money until he utters the fatal aspiration, "I wish to Heaven I was made of money!" The wish involves a curse, and it is accomplished. Jericho's heart turns into a repository of bank notes from which he can freely draw, only each note he removes diminishes his physical dimensions until he is destroyed. Jerrold obviously took the idea for the story from Balzac's *La Peau de Chagrin* (1831) in which Raphael de Valentin, a talented student who is unable to attain the complete satisfaction of his intense soul and senses, is on the verge of suicide when he comes into possession of the small skin of a wild ass, which has the magic power of miraculously granting its owner's wishes—at the price of shortening his life. The skin, which shrinks with every expressed desire, symbolically represents Raphael's ebbing life. By making the supernatural device an integral part of his hero's body, Jerrold makes the image of deterioration even more fantastic, direct, and vivid than Balzac's.

James Hannay rightly calls the story "a kind of bastard-allegory." [42] Jerrold freely juxtaposes realistic details with allegorical abstractions in his portrayal of Jericho. When the story opens, for instance, Jericho is a common man of the common world, a moneymaking, grasping person; and he is henpecked like Job Caudle, who complains to his wife that "bed isn't the place to talk in." Jerrold prepares the reader for the effect of Jericho's fatal wish through his wife, the former widow Pennibacker, whose tongue goads him like a fury into the world of fantasy: "All his life had Jericho trod upon firm earth; but widow Pennibacker whipped him off his leaden feet, and carried him away into the fairy ground of Mammon; and there his eyes twinkled at imaginary wealth, and his ears burned and stood erect at the sound of shaken shadowy money-bags." [43]

After his heart is transmuted, the weird juxtaposition of the fantastic with the ordinary, vain, worldly existence of his wife and daughters is maintained throughout the story. The other characters see his sudden wealth and his survival of a bullet wound in his heart, sustained in a duel, as the result of a pact he had made with the devil. This theme, which one already observed in the short stories, is developed until Jericho, emaciated and isolated with his last few bank notes, is given one of his heart's notes by Plutus, his "devilish serving man," with which to light a candle.

When he puts the bill in the flame, he is consumed to ashes, as are all his past purchases made with the unnaturally gained wealth. The fantastic theme of Jericho's physical and moral deterioration is developed and consummated alongside of the believable theme of the Jericho family's social climbing: Sabilla's purchase of fine dresses for her marriageable daughters, her attempts to marry them to promising parliamentary and aristocratic neighbors, and the acquisition of Jogtrot Hall as a symbol of gentility.

Jericho's opposite is to be found in his stepson, witty and intelligent Basil, who rejects his father's money in order to marry the daughter of the Carraway family, who went bankrupt and lost Jogtrot Hall to the Jerichos. Basil's speech is full of wit, sarcasm, and poetry; his description of Australia, where he plans to live with Bessy Carraway and start a new life, is highly imaginative: "Quite a land of plenty! Earth is here so kind, that just tickle her with a hoe and she laughs with a harvest" (171). Jerrold's characterization of Basil, however, is seriously damaged by a problem of technique. In the first part of the book, he is pictured as a brash youth who resembles Tony Lumpkin in his undisciplined behavior. Later, when Jerrold wants him for a moral foil to Jericho, he cannot make the transformation convincing and becomes involved in an awkward and abrupt shift in point of view. When Basil comes of age, he decides "to strip himself for the race of life, casting aside all needless trappings; all foolish cumbrous pride; all vanities . . ." (139). The incredible change is also complicated by having Basil narrate the story of his twenty-first birthday to his eldest boy, aged eighteen. Since Basil's marriage is only presumed *after* the story closes, the sudden leap into the distant future is an unacceptable intrusion in the narration by the omniscient author. Midway through Basil's account Jerrold interrupts: "the reader, we trust, has not forgotten that Basil is all the while talking in this page by anticipation—compelled to do so by the tyranny of the quill, to his unborn boy Basil, junior" (141).

Even so skilled a stylist as Robert Louis Stevenson had difficulty maintaining a consistent point of view in *Treasure Island,* but one can appreciate the problem involved in having a personal narrator tell of events he could not witness. Jerrold faced that very problem in *The Story of a Feather*. But, since here he is writing as the omniscient narrator, there is no justifiable reason for introducing another narrator who disturbs both the point of view

and the time sequence. The immediacy of personal observation
does not warrant the shift in this instance. Dickens managed a
similar switch from omniscient to personal narrative in *Bleak
House* with more ease and thematic justification, but he failed to
warn the reader beforehand. Jerrold not only warns the reader
but intrudes to remind him who is speaking and to apologize for
the switch.

Basil resembles Jerrold not only in his wit and sarcasm but in
his early unsettled career. Like Jerrold, he planned to be a lawyer
but became a humorist who fears the excesses of humor: "I purpose to start in life as a Comic Undertaker" (99). The conflict
within Jerrold between creating humor for its own sake and
humor with a moral or social message is experienced by Basil as
he sarcastically reflects upon the times:

"It will be my lasting reputation," said Basil, "to meet the grand
desire of the age. For do you not perceive, sir, the great tendency of
our time is to sink the serious, and to save the droll? Folks who have
an eagle in their coat-of-arms begin to be ashamed of it, and paint it
out for the laughing goose. In a very little while and we shall put a
horse-collar about the world, expressly for all the world to grin through
it." (226)

Like Basil, Jerrold experienced a transformation of character
when he ceased writing humorous works such as the *Curtain Lectures* and wanted his reputation to rest upon more serious and
instructive works: *A Man Made of Money, The Story of a Feather,*
and *The Chronicles of Clovernook.*

Throughout Jerrold's career as a journalist, dramatist, and author, he attacked the imperfections of his age. In *The Chronicles
of Clovernook; with Some Account of the Hermit of Bellyfulle* he
presents the imaginative realization of his social ideals in a utopian picture of society. James Stirling recounts Jerrold's pride
in his own work: "He gave me, also, a copy of *Clovernook,*
showing me, with some pride, a translation of it in German, and
expressing the decided opinion that it was his best work." [44] It is
ironic that he wrote this tale full of pastoral scenes and harmoni-
ous contentment at a time when he was racked with rheumatic
pains that grew so severe he had several times to discontinue the
monthly installments of the novel in *The Illuminated Magazine.*

The Chronicles of Clovernook combines the genre of the imaginary journey with the utopian essay. The nineteenth century was later to produce a number of utopian visions both in novels and in essays, and among them were Alexander Smith's "Dreamthorp," Bulwer-Lytton's *The Coming Race*, William Morris' *News From Nowhere*, and Ruskin's *Fors Clavigera*. Jerrold's utopia is not based upon any previous scheme, but one finds a vague resemblance to the Houyhnhnm and Brobdingnag sections of Swift's *Gulliver's Travels*.

The narrator keeps the location of Clovernook a secret in order to preserve it from contamination from the rest of the world and "consecrated to our own delicious leisure, when time runs by like a summer brook, dimpling and sweetly murmuring as it runs." [45] The narrator, who loses his way during a journey, finds himself in the cottage of the Hermit of Bellyfulle, a fat Rabelaisian character who has dedicated his life to writing an encyclopedia of cooking and whose walls are appropriately decorated with sausages and hams. He tells his visitor of his journeys to the utopian lands of As-You-Like and Turveytop, and he explains how the people in Clovernook have come from the everyday world to redeem themselves.

The pastoral setting of Clovernook is described in highly picturesque terms that suggest rural Kent, where Jerrold as a child spent a few years among country sights and sounds before moving away with his family to the turmoil of a busy seaport during the Napoleonic wars. Even the inscription over the hermit's mantelpiece echoes the traditional opening of poems of rural retreat: "Happy is the man who may tell all his dreams" (248). As a man harassed by the business of the city, it seems only natural that Jerrold's utopia should be full of "sweet-smelling shrubs and flowers, orange-trees and heliotropes, and the friendly honey-suckle," where there are paths of herbs that "crushed by our feet sighed forth their odorous breath" (300).

It is the land of "As-You-Like," however, that Jerrold uses as his idealized version of England. The hermit, who was flown there years ago by means of a magic bottle, describes it to his guest. The government is a limited monarchy. The nobles, such as the Duke of Lovingkindness and the Marquis of Sensibility, are full of compassion; their heraldic arms symbolize charity instead of callous pride. The church is deeply reverenced, and the bishops give away all their money to the poor. The House of Lords is called the

House of Virtues, where bishops condemn instead of condone war. The second assembly is called the House of Workers, and "no man could be one of these, who had not made known to the world his wisdom—his justice—his worship of truth for truth's sake" (244). The debates are short, and their laws are plainly worded so that all can understand them. Only one cannon remains from a war fought a thousand years ago, and the swallows now nest in it.

Tradesmen in this ideal state tell their customers the truth about their products and often refuse to sell defective merchandise. The only tax is "the truth-tax," under which every man reports his wealth and goods, and pays in proportion to his substance. Although there are prisons for the idle and vicious, "the state . . . with paternal love, watched . . . at the very cradles of the poor,—teaching the pauper, as he grew, a self-responsibility; showing to him right and wrong . . ." (246). The state also surrounds the people with beautiful objects and the museums, art galleries, and churches were open to all.

All these virtues can be traced directly to the corresponding vices which Jerrold attacked in *Punch*. The closest nineteenth-century successor to Clovernook is Samuel Butler's *Erewhon, or Over the Range* (1872). Like Jerrold, he created his story from articles he had written earlier, such as "Darwin Among the Machines" (1863) and "The World of the Unborn" (1865). Jerrold based some of the background scenes on rural Kent; Butler, on New Zealand. Erewhon, like Clovernook, is described in terms that suggest a pastoral setting: "The country was highly cultivated, every ledge being planted with chestnuts, walnuts, and apple-trees from which the apples were now gathering. Goats were abundant; also a kind of small black cattle, in the marshes near the river . . . I saw a few sheep with rounded noses and enormous tails."

Some of the themes considered by Jerrold are treated again by Butler, and these include his satire of religion in "The Musical Banks," materialistic science in "The Book of the Machines," and the problem of parenthood in "The World of the Unborn." Both authors invert the usual standards of society for satiric effect: the roles of doctors and justices are reversed in Erewhon, where disease and misfortune are considered criminal and moral problems are treated by "straighteners." In Turveytop, so called because "heroes and wise folk of our world become sad lubbers and dunces among the giants," the schoolmaster is considered "the nobility of the people." He must teach the businessman that *good* does not mean *gold*, the rector that it does not mean *pig* (tithing), and the soldier that it does not mean *blood*.

In Butler's myth of the Unborn, pure and simple souls must forget their "gaseous yet more or less anthropomorphic existence" [46] upon entering the world of the born, where they will eventually be sent to the schools of Unreason to acquire hypothetical principles that incapacitate them for society. In Turveytop, however, people who undermine the ideal society—warmongering generals, unscrupulous businessmen, and hypocritical clergymen—become babies again and are re-educated and purged of their "wicked worldliness" by the wise and benevolent giants.

The Hermit describes this process: "Oh! the men I have seen there," cried the Hermit, with a laugh—"the kings, lords, bishops, lawmakers I have seen, all put into second swaddling clothes, and brought up again as gentle, wise, charitable, sagacious folk, doing good credit to the beautiful earth, which, in their former days, they so grievously scandalised" (278).

Turveytop is Jerrold's plea to England to strengthen its educational system; he believed that crime was the result of ignorance and neglect fostered by England's indifference to her poor. Although this concept was also one of the major themes of *St. Giles and St. James*, it is most explicitly stated through the Hermit: "In Turveytop, the schoolmaster is considered the maker of future people—the moral artificer of society. Hence, the state pays him peculiar consideration. It is allowed that his daily labours are in the immortal chambers of the mind; the mind of childhood, new from the Maker's hand, and undefiled by earth. Hence, there is a solemnity, almost a sacredness, in the schoolmaster's function: upon him and his high and tender doings does the state of Turveytop depend, that its prisons shall be few" (285).

Finally, Jerrold expounds in detail his philosophy of the social function of humor, which has already been glimpsed as seen in his journalism and in his stories. He believed laughter was an expression of the divine in man, that it complemented man's sober reasoning faculties and completed his being:

Why, sir, laughter is to the face of man—what sinovia, I think anatomists call it, is to his joints:—it oils, and lubricates, and makes the human countenance divine. Without it, our faces would have been rigid, hyaena-like; the iniquities of our heart, with no sweet antidote to work upon them, would have made the face of the best among us a horrid, husky thing, with two sullen, hungry, cruel lights at the top —for foreheads would have then gone out of fashion—and a cavernous hole below the nose. (289)

The Hermit explains how the God of Laughter averted a civil war in Turveytop waged between his worshipers and their humorless enemies: he turned their guns into sausages and their bullets into candy. Absurd as such an incident is, Jerrold expected its message to be taken seriously; and he affirms that the lack of a sense of humor in English government distorts its ability to act in a completely human and humane fashion. Humor liberates the divinity in man and suffuses his reason, making him compassionate; and Jerrold himself wrote with the sense of a social missionary who brought the gospel of wit and laughter to a society unredeemed in its grim earnestness. His elevated conception of humor resembles Carlyle's theory that he formulated in his essay on Jean Paul Richter:

> True humour springs not more from the head than from the heart; it is not contempt, its essence is love; it issues not in laughter, but in still smiles, which lie deeper. It is a sort of inverse sublimity; exalting, as it were, into our affections what is below us, while sublimity draws down into our affections what is above us. The former is scarcely less precious or heart-affecting than the latter; perhaps it is still rarer, and, as a test of genius, still more decisive. It is, in fact, the bloom and perfume, the purest effluence of a deep, fine and loving nature; a nature in harmony with itself, reconciled to the world and its stintedness and contradiction, nay, finding in this very contradiction new elements of beauty as well as goodness.[47]

Both Carlyle and Jerrold take humor seriously and consider it an expression of love or compassion; for Carlyle, it is "a sort of inverse sublimity"; for Jerrold, it is a kind of "divinity."

The fairyland of Clovernook—the stepping stone to Turveytop and As-You-Like—will continue to exist, says Jerrold, despite "the real world gaol locked and grated by Mulciber Convention"; and, "though a thing of dreams," Clovernook is "far more enduring than the bricks of Babylon" (344).

CHAPTER 5

Conclusion

IN the light of Jerrold's diverse talents as journalist, playwright, novelist, editor, essayist, and wit, it is surprising that he has been almost completely neglected in recent studies of the Victorian age. He has often been mentioned as a friend of Thackeray and Dickens, but his close alliance with them as an early and influential literary force has not been explored. Nevertheless, it has been seen that, as a co-worker for *Punch*, Thackeray was not only envious of Jerrold's popularity but joined him in his attack upon snobbery and apparently modeled his "Titmarsh" papers upon Jerrold's "Papers of a Gentleman-at-Arms." His influence upon Dickens is also apparent in *Sketches by Boz* and in *A Christmas Carol*. Considering the very close friendship between the two men and the fidelity and admiration with which Dickens read Jerrold's works, one cannot ignore the evidence of mutual influences.

It is hardly necessary to point out that Jerrold's plays have no place in the modern theater; they are not serious works of art. On the other hand, they are first-rate melodramas and, when transformed from the printed page to the theater, his plays could doubtless still elicit laughter from the sober audience. Even more than most forms of the drama, farce and melodrama seem to require the magic of lights, setting, costume, and skilled actors for their success. They are also interesting for their revelation of popular taste and convention and for their role in the evolution of the melodrama into the new theater of Pinero and Shaw. Similarly, Jerrold's novels are of more concern to the literary historian than to the modern reader seeking entertainment and illumination.

Nevertheless, even in the areas of fiction and drama, literary historians have not accorded Jerrold sufficient acknowledgement. This neglect may be due in part to the absence of critical studies and readily available editions of his works that would provide a sound basis for an estimate of his merit. *The Cambridge History of English Literature* (1907–27), Ernest Baker's *A History of the English Novel* (1924–39), and Albert Baugh's *A Literary History of England* (1948), for example, take their descriptions of Jerrold's works and their comments about his achievements from either M. H. Spielmann's *History of Punch* (1895) or Walter Jerrold's *Douglas Jerrold, Dramatist and Wit.* Today, it is time that opinions formulated over seventy years ago be revised in the light of more objective criticism. Jerrold certainly merits more than the half sentence accorded him by Oliver Elton in *A Survey of English Literature* (1920) and at least deserves to be discussed on a level with Thomas Hood, Dion Boucicault, and Lewis Carroll.

Jerrold, as Mr. Punch—attacking the status quo, setting Thackeray's teeth on edge, stirring French antipathy, and lampooning the professional practitioners of cant and humbug—shines at his best. Not only may the literary historian discover a powerful satiric force at work in the world of *Punch,* but anyone today can find lively reading in *Mrs. Caudle's Curtain Lectures, The English in Little,* or *Punch's Letters to His Son.* The whole concept of comic journalism as a distinct genre, worthy of careful study, has been ignored in recent scholarship. Too often the trade of journalism has been viewed merely as an apprenticeship grimly undertaken by promising novelists who, after they develop a distinctive style, graduate to the respectable world of novels. Perhaps because Jerrold himself felt this way, he made his awkward attempt to follow in the path of Thackeray and Dickens. But Jerrold was a pioneer in the new genre of comic journalism; and, as its foremost expositor, Jerrold surpasses his contemporaries and successfully communicates his humor to the present age. No discussion of Victorian humor can be complete that does not take into account the satire, wit, parody, and burlesque of Douglas Jerrold.

Notes and References

Chapter One

1. "Bajazet Gag; the Manager in Search of a 'Star,'" *New Monthly Magazine*, LXIV n.s. (1842), 189.
2. Quoted in Walter Jerrold, *Douglas Jerrold, Dramatist and Wit* (2 vols.; London, 1914), I, 22.
3. *Ibid.*, p. 59.
4. *Ibid.*, p. 150.
5. *Ibid.*, p. 265.
6. *The Writings of Douglas Jerrold* (8 vols.; London, 1851–58), VIII, 199.
7. W. Jerrold, *Douglas Jerrold, Dramatist and Wit*, II, 142.
8. Gordon N. Ray, *Thackeray: The Uses of Adversity, 1811–1846* (New York, 1955), p. 355.
9. Quoted in W. Jerrold, *Douglas Jerrold, Dramatist and Wit*, II, 527.
10. Quoted in Ray, *Thackeray: The Uses of Adversity*, p. 355.
11. Quoted in W. Jerrold, *Douglas Jerrold, Dramatist and Wit*, I, 176.
12. Quoted in Ray, *Thackeray: The Uses of Adversity*, p. 355.
13. Quoted in W. Blanchard Jerrold, *The Life of Douglas Jerrold* (Philadelphia and London, n.d.), p. 248.
14. Quoted in W. Jerrold, *Douglas Jerrold, Dramatist and Wit*, II, 473.
15. *Ibid.*, pp. 518, 520.
16. *Ibid.*, p. 599.
17. Nathaniel Hawthorne, *Notes of Travel* (4 vols.; New York, 1900), II, 92.

Chapter Two

1. *The Writings of Douglas Jerrold*, VIII, 269.
2. Jo Helen Railsback, "The Thomas Becket Story as a Theme in Dramatic Literature," Diss. University of Tennessee, 1969, pp. 100–113.

3. Quoted in *Douglas Jerrold, Dramatist and Wit*, I, 193–94.
4. *The Writings of Douglas Jerrold*, VIII, 43.
5. *Ibid.*, VII, 228–29.
6. Quoted in W. Blanchard Jerrold, *The Life of Douglas Jerrold*, p. 162.
7. *The Writings of Douglas Jerrold*, VII, 156, 195.
8. *Ibid.*, p. 171.

Chapter Three

1. *The Letters and Private Papers of William Makepeace Thackeray*, ed. Gordan N. Ray (4 vols.; Cambridge, 1945–46), IV, 48.
2. M. H. Spielmann, *The History of Punch* (New York, 1895), p. 284.
3. See Ray, *Thackeray: The Uses of Adversity*, pp. 355, 362, 363.
4. Henry Vizetelly, *Glances Back Through Seventy Years* (2 vols.; London, 1893), I, 290.
5. Ray, *Thackeray: The Uses of Adversity*, p. 369.
6. Ray (ed.), *The Letters and Private Papers of William Makepeace Thackeray*, II, 274.
7. R. G. G. Price, *A History of Punch* (London, 1957), p. 30.
8. Spielmann, *The History of Punch*, p. 6.
9. "The Moral of Punch," *Punch*, I (1841), 1.
10. "Punch, Member for the City of London," *Punch*, V (1843), 148.
11. Spielmann, *The History of Punch*, p. 100.
12. "Parliament and Peel's Victim," *Punch*, VI (1844), 58.
13. "Punch's Court Calendar," *Punch*, IV (1843), 252.
14. "A Dainty Dish to Set Before a Queen," *Punch*, IX (1845), 135.
15. "The Queen in Scotland," *Punch*, VII (1844), 146.
16. James Hutchinson Stirling, *Jerrold, Tennyson and Macaulay* (Edinburgh, 1868), p. 35.
17. Quoted in Walter Jerrold, *Douglas Jerrold and 'Punch'* (London, 1910), p. 45.
18. "The 'Weight' of Royalty.—The Social 'Scale,'" *Punch*, I (1841), 270.
19. This letter appeared in *The Times* (Jan. 12, 1843), p. 5, addressed to W. Barlow: "Sir,—I was not aware, until to-day, that the specimen of manufacture which you requested me to accept bore any allusion to matters that are the subject of public controversy. No mention whatever was made of this in the letter you addressed to me; and I thought it would be ungracious to reject what appeared to be a pure act of civility on your part. I must beg leave to return to you that which I accepted under an erroneous impression. I am, Sir, your obedient servant,—Robert Peel."

This letter is followed by Barlow's disclamation of any intention on his part of connecting Peel's acceptance of the velveteen with any subject of public controversy.

20. "Peel's 'Velveteens,' " *Punch*, IV (1843), 36.

21. This idea may have suggested Thackeray's *Mr. Punch's Prize Novelists* (1847).

22. "Prize Preface," *Punch*, VI (1844), iii.

23. " 'Gentlemen Jews,' " *Punch*, VI (1844), 79.

24. " 'Gentlemen Jews' and Punch," *Punch*, VI (1844), 104.

25. "The Wrongs of Punch.—His Expulsion from France," *Punch*, IV (1843), 75.

26. "Wanted.—A Few Bold Smugglers!" *Punch*, VII (1844), 106.

27. "The Frenchmen in Algiers.—Lovely War!" *Punch*, IX (1845), 44.

28. "The Emperor of Russia's Visit to England," *Punch*, VI (1844), 144.

29. "Nicholas and the Jews," *Punch*, VII (1844), 166.

30. "Nicholas Snubbed," *Punch*, X (1846), 25.

31. Charles and Mary Cowden Clarke, "Douglas Jerrold and His Letters," *The Gentleman's Magazine*, n.s. 6, XVII (1876), 507.

32. Quoted in W. Jerrold, *Douglas Jerrold, Dramatist and Wit*, II, 528.

33. *Ibid.*, p. 599.

34. "American Liberty.—American Eggs," *Punch*, XIII (1847), 154.

35. "The President and the Negro," *Punch*, VI (1844), 155.

36. "The President's Oath," *Punch*, VIII (1845), 160.

37. "War with America," *Punch*, X (1846), 71.

38. *The English in Little*, *Punch*, XI (1846), 195, 199, 211, 219, 235, 239, 257, 264; XII (1847), 1, 19, 39, 63, 95, 162. The installments appeared on a regular weekly basis between Nov. 7, 1846, and Jan. 9, 1847. The last three installments appeared on Feb. 13, March 6, and April 17, 1847. All future references are indicated in the text by volume and page number.

39. Anthony Trollope, *Thackeray* (London, 1925), p. 82.

40. J. Y. T. Greig, *Thackeray, A Reconsideration* (London, 1950), p. 90.

41. "The May-Day of Steam," *Punch*, VI (1844), 196.

42. "The 'Milk' of Poor-Law 'Kindness,' " *Punch*, IV (1843), 46.

43. "The Moral of Punch," *Punch*, I (1841), 1.

44. "Old Bailey Justice After Dinner," *Punch*, VII (1844), 219.

45. *The Letters of Charles Dickens*, ed. Walter Dexter (3 vols.; Bloomsbury, 1938), I, 517.

46. *Ibid.*, p. 638.

47. Quoted in Walter Jerrold, *Douglas Jerrold, Dramatist and Wit*, I, 212.

48. Thackeray, "Mr. Leech's Sketches in Oil," the *Times* (June 2, 1862), p. 5.

49. *Times* (Nov. 3, 1841), p. 7.

50. "Sir Peter Laurie on Human Life," *Punch*, I (1841), 210.

51. "The Pig-Skin Solomon," *Punch*, IV (1843), 206.

52. "Beauties and Beasts," *Punch*, XV (1848), 125.

53. *The Works of Charles Dickens* (34 vols.; London, 1897–99), XVII, 127.

54. "Going to See a Man Hanged," *Fraser's Magazine*, XXII (Aug. 1840), 156.

55. "The Moral of Punch," *Punch*, I (1841), 1.

56. "The Hangman's 'Moral Lessons,' " *Punch*, VIII (1845), 151.

57. "Blood," *Punch*, II (1842), 190.

58. "Old Bailey Blossoms," *Punch*, VIII (1845), 177–78.

59. *The Writings of Douglas Jerrold*, V, 92–94, 140–47.

60. "Sisters of Misery," *Punch*, XV (1848), 78.

61. "The Reconcilation: a Prophecy by Punch," *Punch*, VIII (1845), 122.

62. Sir Nathaniel, "Notes on Note-Worthies," CX (1857), 414.

63. Thackeray, in *The Morning Chronicle* (Dec. 26, 1845), p. 5.

64. *Emilia Wyndham* (3 vols.; London, 1846), I, 76–77.

65. *Ibid.*, III, 360.

66. "Punch's Review," *Punch*, X (1846), 269.

67. *The Writings of Douglas Jerrold*, III, vi.

The nagging wife can be heard as early as the mystery play *Noah*. In the *Canterbury Tales* the Wife of Bath glories in her triumphs over her various husbands, and Pertelote lectures Chaunticleer on his dreams.

The literary tradition of the curtain lecture goes back to the seventeenth century. In 1637 Thomas Heywood published *A Curtaine Lecture*, composed of several short tales about shrewish wives' mistreatment of their husbands. Richard Brathwaite attacked Heywood's book, along with several others of a similar nature, in his *Ar't Asleepe Husband?* (1640). Although he also relates stories about shrewish wives, his purpose is to bring about by contrast the noble virtues of womankind. Opposite the title page is a picture of a wife lecturing her husband in bed, and below the drawing are these lines, suggestive of the Caudles:

> This Wife a wondrous racket meanes to keepe,
> While th'husband seemes to sleepe but do'es not sleepe:
> But she might full as well her lecture smother,
> For ent'ring one eare, it goes out t'other.

Presumably the practice of curtain lecturing was well established by the eighteenth century, where the art appears in *Tatler* No. 243, and its typical practitioner underlies the characters of Mrs. Oakly (George Colman, *The Jealous Wife*), Lady Teazle (Richard Sheridan, *The School for Scandal*), Mrs. Partridge (Henry Fielding, *Tom Jones*), Mrs. Primrose (Oliver Goldsmith, *The Vicar of Wakefield*), and Mrs. Baynard (Tobias Smollett, *Humphry Clinker*). Jane Collier's *Essay on the Art of Ingeniously Tormenting* (1755) finally formularizes the proper psychological rules by which a wife may torture her husband and vice versa. But none of the husbands in the works mentioned above is as long-suffering as Job Caudle and none of their wives is as completely overpowering and persistent as Mrs. Caudle, the only one of her type that stands out as a success in the first forty years of the nineteenth century.

68. Thackeray, in *The Morning Chronicle* (December 26, 1845), p. 5.

69. *Mrs. Caudle's Curtain Lectures, The Writings of Douglas Jerrold*, III, 72. Subsequent references to the work will be indicated in the text as *CL*, if another reference intervenes; otherwise, only page numbers are cited.

70. Sarah Ellis, *The Wives of England. Their Relative Duties, Domestic Influence, and Social Obligations* (New York, 1843), p. 4.

71. John Ruskin, "Of Queens' Gardens," *Sesame and Lilies* (London, n.d.), p. 59.

72. Ellis, *The Wives of England*, pp. 99–100.

73. Ruskin, "Of Queens' Gardens," p. 60.

74. Quoted in Janet Dunbar, *The Early Victorian Woman* (London, 1953), pp. 18, 19.

75. Ellis, *The Wives of England*, p. 38.

76. C. Willett Cunnington, *Feminine Attitudes in the Nineteenth Century* (New York, 1936), pp. 109–10.

77. "The Momentous Question," *Punch*, IX (1845), 183.

78. Ellis, *The Wives of England*, p. 112.

79. Thackeray, in *The Morning Chronicle* (Dec. 26, 1845), p. 5.

80. *Ibid.*

81. *Punch's Letters to His Son, The Writings of Douglas Jerrold*, V, 5. Subsequent references to this work will be indicated in the text as *PLS* if another reference intervenes; otherwise, only page references are given.

82. *Letters Written by the Earl of Chesterfield to His Son* (Philadelphia, 1833), p. 233. Subsequent references to this work will be indicated in the text as *CLS*, if another reference intervenes; otherwise, only page numbers are cited.

83. For the discussion which follows I have used Walter Jerrold,

Douglas Jerrold and 'Punch', (London, 1910), which contains a reprint of the above serial along with *Capsicum House for Young Ladies, Our Honeymoon,* and *Exhibition of the English in China;* and Daniel Defoe, *Robinson Crusoe* (New York, 1948). Subsequent references to *The Life and Adventures of Miss Robinson Crusoe* will be indicated in the text as *MRC* if another reference intervenes; otherwise, only page references are given.

84. Defoe, *Robinson Crusoe* (New York, 1848), p. 56. Subsequent references to this work will be indicated in the text as *RC* if another reference intervenes; otherwise, only page references are given.

85. Quoted in Janet Dunbar, *The Early Victorian Woman,* p. 34.

86. Thackeray, *Vanity Fair* (New York, 1955), p. 2.

87. *Capsicum House for Young Ladies, Douglas Jerrold and 'Punch',* p. 143. Subsequent page references to this work will be indicated in the text.

88. Ruskin, "Of Queens' Gardens," p. 61.

89. C. Willett Cunnington, *Feminine Attitudes in the Nineteenth Century,* p. 109.

Chapter Four

1. "Job Pippins: the Man who 'Couldn't Help It,'" *The Writings of Douglas Jerrold,* II, 8.

2. *Ibid.,* V, 267.

3. *Ibid.,* p. 268.

4. Henry Vizetelly, *Glances Back Through Seventy Years* (2 vols.; London, 1893), I, 324–25.

5. "The 'Post' at the Opera," *Punch,* IV (1843), 126.

6. "Jenkins on 'Society,'" *Punch,* IV (1843), 206.

7. [Review of *Adelia*] *The Morning Post* (March 13, 1843), p. 5.

8. "The 'Post' at the Opera," *Punch,* IV (1843), 126.

9. "Nettles," *Punch,* IV (1843), 176.

10. "The Jenkins' 'Nettles,'" *Punch,* IV (1843), 196.

11. "Something From, and of, 'Jenkins,'" *Punch,* IV (1843), 216.

12. Vizetelly, *Glances Back Through Seventy Years,* I, 324.

13. "The Perennial Jenkins!," *Punch,* V (1843), 43.

14. Thackeray, "Punch's Parting Tribute to Jenkins," *Punch,* V (1843), 123.

15. Thackeray, "Gems from Jenkins," *Punch,* VI (1844), 153.

16. Vizetelly, *Glances Back Through Seventy Years,* I, 325.

17. "Jenkins!," *Punch,* VI (1844), 188.

18. *The Sick Giant and the Doctor Dwarf, The Writings of Douglas Jerrold,* III, 307–22.

19. *The Brownrigg Papers,* ed. Blanchard Jerrold (London, 1860), p. 282.

20. Jerrold was known to Poe through a friend, Richard Hengist Horne, who, in 1844, wrote to Poe that he could place his tale, "The Spectacles," in the *Illuminated Magazine,* but Poe chose not to because neither the circulation nor the remuneration would be adequate. See Walter Jerrold, *Douglas Jerrold, Dramatist and Wit,* II, 362, 363. The Poe literature makes no mention of Jerrold on this point. Killis Campbell (*The Mind of Poe and Other Studies* [Cambridge, 1933]) claims Balzac's story "La Grande Bretèche" (1830) suggested Poe's tale. Joseph S. Shick, however, says Poe's sources were Joel Tyler Headley's *Letters From Italy* (1845) and Bulwer-Lytton's *The Last Days of Pompeii* ("The Origin of the 'Cask of Amontillado,'" *American Literature,* VI, 18–21). Although *Letters From Italy* contains the most resemblances to Poe's tale, like the other suggested sources, it makes no mention of a wine cellar as the place of burial.

21. *The Handbook of Swindling, and other Papers,* ed. Walter Jerrold (London, n.d.), pp. 165, 168.

22. R. H. Barham, *The Ingoldsby Legends or Mirth and Marvels* (New York, n.d.), p. 229.

23. "The Mayor of Hole-Cum-Corner," *The Writings of Douglas Jerrold,* IV, 108.

24. "Ephraim Rue: the 'Victim of Society,'" *New Monthly Magazine,* LXII, n.s. (1841), 213.

25. "Mr. Peppercorn at Home," *The Writings of Douglas Jerrold,* IV, 153–60.

26. "The Lesson of Life," *The Writings of Douglas Jerrold,* IV, 85.

27. Allardyce Nicoll, *Early Nineteenth Century Drama, 1800–1850* (Cambridge, 1955), pp. 186–87.

28. "The Preacher Parrot," *The Writings of Douglas Jerrold,* IV, 202.

29. "The Papers of a 'Gentleman-at-Arms,'" *New Monthly Magazine,* LIII n.s. (1838), 95, 98, 248.

30. Thackeray, "Memorials of Gormandising," *Fraser's Magazine,* XXIII (1841), 710.

31. "The Papers of a 'Gentleman-at-Arms,'" *New Monthly Magazine,* LIV (1838), 108, 117.

32. W. Blanchard Jerrold, *The Life of Douglas Jerrold* (London, n.d.), p. 209. This letter is not in Dexter.

33. Andrew Block, in his catalogue of novels, lists an anonymous story, published in 1812, entitled *The Adventures of an Ostrich Feather of Quality* (*The English Novel* [London, 1961]). Jerrold possibly derived his idea from this work.

34. *The Story of a Feather, The Writings of Douglas Jerrold,* III, 205, 263. Subsequent references to this work are indicated in the text.

35. W. Blanchard Jerrold, *The Life of Douglas Jerrold*, p. 209.

36. *St. Giles and St. James, The Writings of Douglas Jerrold*, I, iii-iv. Subsequent references to this work are indicated in the text.

37. Sir Nathaniel, "Notes on Note-Worthies," *New Monthly Magazine*, CX (1857), 411.

38. *St. Giles and St. James, Douglas Jerrold's Shilling Magazine*, V (1847), 469.

39. [Anon. review of *A Man Made of Money*] *Athenaeum* (1848), p. 1000.

40. [Anon. review of *A Man Made of Money*] *Athenaeum* (1854), p. 1295.

41. James Hannay, "Douglas Jerrold," *The Atlantic Monthly Magazine*, I (Nov., 1857), 9.

42. *Ibid.*, p. 8.

43. *A Man Made of Money, The Writings of Douglas Jerrold*, VI, 8. Subsequent references to this work are indicated in the text.

44. Quoted in Walter Jerrold, *Douglas Jerrold, Dramatist and Wit*, I, 429.

45. *The Chronicles of Clovernook, The Writings of Douglas Jerrold*, VI, 232. Subsequent references to this work will be indicated in the text.

46. *The Works of Samuel Butler*, eds. H. F. Jones and A. T. Bartholomew (20 vols.; London, 1923–26), II, 46, 142.

47. Thomas Carlyle, "Jean Paul Friedrich Richter," *Critical and Miscellaneous Essays* (5 vols.; London, 1899) I, 17.

Selected Bibliography

Writings by Jerrold

1. Editions of Jerrold's Works

   The Best of Mr. Punch: the Humorous Writings of Douglas Jerrold. Ed. Richard M. Kelly. Knoxville: University of Tennessee Press, 1970.

   The Works of Douglas Jerrold. With an introductory memoir by his son, W. Blanchard Jerrold. 5 Vols. London: Bradbury and Evans, n.d.

   The Writings of Douglas Jerrold (Collected Edition). 8 Vols. London: Bradbury and Evans, 1851–58.

2. Miscellaneous Collections

   Bon-mots of Charles Lamb and Douglas Jerrold. Ed. Walter Jerrold. London: J. M. Dent and Co., 1893.

   The Brownrigg Papers. Ed. Blanchard Jerrold. London: J. C. Hotten, 1860.

   Clarke, Charles and Mary Cowden. "Douglas Jerrold and His Letters," *The Gentleman's Magazine,* XVII, n.s. 6 (1876). Several letters are reprinted that corroborate Jerrold's sympathy with Mazzini.

   Douglas Jerrold and 'Punch'. London: Macmillan and Co., 1910. Part I by Walter Jerrold; Part II reprints *Capsicum House for Young Ladies, The Life and Adventures of Miss Robinson Crusoe, Our Honeymoon,* and *Exhibition of the English in China.*

   Douglas Jerrold's Shilling Magazine. Edited by Douglas Jerrold. 7 Vols. London, Jan., 1845—June, 1848. Contains *St. Giles and St. James* and numerous essays by Jerrold never reprinted.

   Fireside Saints, Mr. Caudle's Breakfast Talk, and other Papers. Boston: Lee and Shepard, 1888.

The Handbook of Swindling, and Other Papers. Ed., with an introduction, by Walter Jerrold. London: Scott, n.d.

The Illuminated Magazine. Edited by Douglas Jerrold (1843–44) and William John Linton (1844–45). 4 Vols. London, 1843–1845. Contains *The Chronicles of Clovernook* and many editorials and essays by Jerrold that have never been reprinted.

Plays. 2 Vols. Separately bound. London: Thomas Hailes Lacey, n.d.

3. Articles and Stories by Jerrold Not Reprinted (Arranged according to periodicals)

Athenaeum

"The Poulterer's Hare" (Nov. 12, 1831), p. 739.
"Board of Morals" (Nov. 26, 1831), p. 770.
"Thoughts *In* the Pillory" (Dec. 17, 1831), p. 818.
"A Pantomine Club" (Jan. 7, 1832), p. 16.
"A Scene in the Shades" (Feb. 4, 1832), p. 81.
"The Walnut Tree" (March 24, 1832), p. 192.
"The Law of Dramatic Copyright" (April 7, 1832), p. 225.
"Nothing But Rags" (July 7, 1832), p. 441.
"Butcher! Baker!" (Aug. 25, 1832), p. 551.
"Time's Laconics" (Dec. 28, 1833), p. 897.

Bentley's Miscellany

"Mr. Makepeace, the Duellist," XL (1842), 461–66.

Blackwood's Magazine

"Silas Fleshpots; a 'Respectable Man,'" XXXVII (1835), 595–604.
"Michael Lynx; 'the Man Who Knew Himself,'" XXXVII (1835), 730–38.
"An Old House in the City," XXXVII (1835), 860–74.
"The Science of Swindling," XXXVIII (1835), 304–12.
"Isaac Cheek; the 'Man of Wax'," XL (1836), 49–62, 340–70.

New Monthly Magazine

"The 'Lord of Peiresc'," LI n.s. (1837), 177–85.
"Some Account of the Last Parachute," LI n.s. (1837), 250–54.
"Shakespeare's Crab Tree," LVI n.s. (1839), 88.
"The Metaphysician and the Maid," LVI n.s. (1839), 104–20.
"Ephraim Rue; the 'Victim of Society'," LXII n.s. (1841), 212–27.
"Bajazet Gag; the Manager in Search of a 'Star'," LXII n.s. (1841), 369–90, 522–41; LXIII n.s. (1841), 82–99, 337–56, 489–502; LXIV n.s. (1842), 177–92.

Illuminated Magazine

"Elizabeth and Victoria," I (1843), 3–8.
"The Button Holder," I (1843), 54–56, 178–79.
"The Peerage of the Pen," I (1843), 161–64.

Punch

Jerrold's contributions to *Punch* are too extensive to be listed here. For the most complete record of his publications in that journal see the bibliography in Walter Jerrold's *Douglas Jerrold and 'Punch'* and the daybook for *Punch*, a microfilm copy of which is in the University of Tennessee Library.

Writings by Other Authors

BARHAM, RICHARD HARRIS. *The Ingoldsby Legends or Mirth and Marvels*. New York: Worthington, n.d. A clear example of the cult of the comic-grotesque, relevant to Jerrold's "The Wine Cellar."

BRATHWAITE, RICHARD. *Ar't Asleepe Husband?* London: Printed by R. Bishop for Richard Best, 1640. An early analogue of *Mrs. Caudle's Curtain Lectures*.

CHESTERFIELD, EARL OF. *Letters Written by the Earl of Chesterfield to His Son*. Philadelphia: Desilver & Thomas, 1833. The basis of Jerrold's parody, *Punch's Letters to His Son*.

DEFOE, DANIEL. *Robinson Crusoe*. New York: Random House, 1948. Jerrold parodies in *Miss Robinson Crusoe*.

DICKENS, CHARLES. *The Letters of Charles Dickens*. Edited by Walter Dexter. 3 Vols. Bloomsbury, London: Nonesuch Press, 1938. Contains several letters to Jerrold.

HAWTHORNE, NATHANIEL. *The Complete Writings of Nathaniel Hawthorne*. 22 Vols. New York: Houghton, Mifflin & Co., 1900. In his American diary, Hawthorne tells of meeting Jerrold.

HEYWOOD, THOMAS. *A Curtaine Lecture*. London: Printed for John Aston, 1637. One of the earliest analogues of *Mrs. Caudle's Curtain Lectures* and perhaps the first printed use of the phrase "curtain lecture."

HOOK, THEODORE. *Sayings and Doings; or Sketches From Life*. London: H. Colburn, 1824–1828. Influenced Jerrold's tales and character sketches.

LEMON, MARK. "The Moral of Punch," *Punch*, I (1841), 1. Announces the magazine's platform of social satire.

MARSH-CALDWELL, MRS. ANNE. *Emilia Wyndham*. 3 Vols. London: H. Colburn, 1846. Interesting for its defense of womankind and attack upon Jerrold as an anti-feminist.

RUSKIN, JOHN. *Sesame and Lilies*. London and New York: Platt and Peck Co., n.d. Reveals an aspect of Victorian idealization of of married women and the home.

THACKERAY, WILLIAM MAKEPEACE. "Gems From Jenkins," *Punch*, VI (1844), 153. A contribution to Jerrold's attack upon the *Morning Post*.

————. "Going to See a Man Hanged," *Fraser's Magazine*, XXII (Aug., 1840), 150–58. An essay influential among advocates of the abolition of capital punishment; Jerrold and Dickens furthered the crusade.

————. *The Letters and Private Papers of William Makepeace Thackeray*. Edited by Gordon N. Ray. 4 Vols. Cambridge, Mass.: Harvard University Press, 1945–46. Contains much valuable information about Thackeray's relationship to Jerrold.

————. "Punch's Parting Tribute to Jenkins," *Punch*, V (1843), 123. Thackeray's last paper attacking the *Morning Post*.

————. *Thackeray's Contributions to the Morning Chronicle*. Edited by Gordon N. Ray. Urbana: University of Illinois Press, 1955. Contains some material on Jerrold, including Thackeray's review of *Mrs. Caudle's Curtain Lectures*.

————. "Mr. Leech's Sketches in Oil," *The Times* (June 2, 1862), p. 5. Digresses to a perceptive discussion of Jerrold's radicalism in *Punch*.

SECONDARY SOURCES

The following list of works is highly selective. See the Notes and References section for such minor entries as reviews of Jerrold's works, etc.

1. Biographies of Jerrold

JERROLD, WALTER. *Douglas Jerrold, Dramatist and Wit*. 2 Vols. London: Hodder and Stroughton, 1914. The most accurate account of Jerrold's life; invaluable for theatrical material.

Jerrold, W. Blanchard. *The Life of Douglas Jerrold*. Vol. V in the *Works of Douglas Jerrold*. London: Bradbury, Evans and Co., n.d. Important source of biographical data; often marred by factual errors and sentimentality.

2. Miscellaneous Secondary Sources

CLARKE, CHARLES AND MARY COWDEN. *Recollections of Writers*. New York: C. Scribner's Sons, 1878. Section devoted to Jerrold is chatty and anecdotal.

CUNNINGTON, C. WILLETT. *Feminine Attitudes in the Nineteenth*

Century. New York: Macmillan, 1936. The typical Victorian female depicted here serves as an illuminating contrast to Jerrold's comic portrayal of her.

DODDS, JOHN W. *The Age of Paradox.* New York: Rinehart, 1952. Lively account of the Victorian period that provides a valuable background for Jerrold's sweeping satire of current events.

DUNBAR, JANET. *The Early Victorian Woman.* London: Harrap, 1953. Informative and amusing portrait; helpful in understanding Jerrold's satire in *Mrs. Caudle's Curtain Lectures* and *Miss Robinson Crusoe.*

ELLIS, MRS. SARAH. *The Wives of England. Their Relative Duties, Domestic Influence, and Social Obligations.* New York: J. & H. G. Langley, 1843. Standard conduct manual often parodied by Jerrold.

FORSTER, JOHN. *Life of Charles Dickens.* 2 Vols. New York: Baker and Taylor Co., 1911. Contains scattered accounts of Dickens' friendship with Jerrold.

FYVIE, JOHN. "A Forgotten Jester," *Macmillan's Magazine,* LXXXVII (1903), 382–89. Belated, non-critical attempt to revive interest in Jerrold.

"Genius and Writings of Douglas Jerrold," anon. *The Eclectic Magazine,* XXXII (1854), 166–75. Reprinted from the *Eclectic Review.* Laudatory survey of Jerrold's writings and wit.

GOMBRICH, E. H. "The Cartoonist's Armory," *The South Atlantic Quarterly,* LXII (1963), 189–228. Perceptive discussion of caricature that indirectly throws light upon techniques in *Punch.*

HANNAY, JAMES. "Douglas Jerrold," *The Atlantic Monthly Magazine,* I (Nov., 1857), 1–12. The magazine's first essay and one which introduced Jerrold to Americans.

KELLY, RICHARD M. "The American in England: An Examination of a Hitherto Neglected Satire by Douglas Jerrold," *Victorian Newsletter* (Spring, 1967), pp. 28–31. A critical commentary on *The English in Little.*

———. "Chesterfield's *Letters to His Son:* the Victorian Judgment," *Tennessee Studies in Literature,* XV (1970), 109–123. A study of the Victorian response to Chesterfield's *Letters;* includes a discussion of Jerrold's *Punch's Letters to His Son.*

———. "The Jenkins Papers: Douglas Jerrold and William Makepeace Thackeray," *Satire Newsletter,* VIII (1970), 10–15. A commentary on Jerrold's and Thackeray's satire of the *Morning Post.*

———. "Mrs. Caudle, a Victorian Curtain Lecturer," *University* of *Toronto Quarterly*, XXXVIII (1969), 295–309. A study of *Mrs. Caudle's Curtain Lectures.*

————. "Punch's Letters to His Son," *Satire Newsletter,* IV (1967), 58–62. A discussion of Jerrold's serial as a parody of Chesterfield's *Letters to His Son.*

MARCHAND, LESLIE. *The Athenaeum.* Chapel Hill: University of North Carolina Press, 1941. Mentions some of Jerrold's contributions.

MASON, EDWARD TUCKERMAN, ED. *Personal Traits of British Authors.* New York: Charles Scribner's Sons, 1885. Contains some superficial accounts of Jerrold's character.

MAYHEW, ATHOL. *A Jorum of "Punch."* London: Downey & Co., 1895. Informal and informative, though not always accurate, account of the organizers of and early writers for *Punch.*

NATHANIEL, SIR. (pseud.) "Notes on Note-Worthies," *New Monthly Magazine,* n.s. CX (1857), 404–17. The most objective and perceptive criticism of Jerrold by one of his contemporaries.

NICOLL, ALLARDYCE. *Early Nineteenth Century Drama, 1800–1850.* Cambridge: Cambridge University Press, 1955. Bibliography lists all of Jerrold's known plays.

POWELL, THOMAS. *The Living Authors of England.* New York: D. Appleton & Co., 1849. Contains a sketchy account of Jerrold's character.

Price, R. G. G. *A History of Punch.* London: Collins, 1957. Very readable history that brings Spielmann's work up to date.

RAILSBACK, JO HELEN. "The Thomas Becket Story as a Theme in Dramatic Literature." Unpublished dissertation, University of Tennessee, Knoxville, 1969. Contains an analysis of Jerrold's play *Thomas à Becket.*

RAY, GORDON N. *Thackeray: The Uses of Adversity, 1811–1846.* New York: McGraw-Hill, 1955. Clarifies Jerrold's relationship with Thackeray during their years with *Punch.*

SPIELMANN, M. H. *The History of Punch.* New York: Cassell Publishing Co., 1895. Definitive work for the first fifty-four years of *Punch's* development.

STIRLING, JAMES HUTCHINSON. *Jerrold, Tennyson and Macaulay.* Edinburgh: Edmonston & Douglas, 1868. Sympathetic portrayal of Jerrold's character and writings.

STODDARD, RICHARD HENRY, ED. *Personal Reminiscences by Barham, Harness, and Hodder.* New York: Scribner, Armstrong and Co., 1875. Contains some anecdotal material on Jerrold.

The Times (Nov. 3, 1841), p. 7. Alderman Laurie's condemnation of William Simmons.

VIZETELLY, HENRY. *Glances Back Through Seventy Years.* 2 Vols. London: K. Paul, Trench, Trübner and Co., 1893. Although chatty and discursive, contains much information about Jerrold found nowhere else.

Index

(The works of Douglas Jerrold are listed under his name)